Once Upon a Time in Aleppo

Lynne Grant

Published by Marina Leybourne, 2023.

ONCE UPON A TIME IN ALEPPO

First edition. July 9, 2023.

ISBN: 979-8215419687

Written by Lynne Grant.

Table of Contents

To all my friends who made my time in Syria such an amazing experience

Introduction

This is a story about daily life in a Christian community in Aleppo, Syria in the 1990s. All the events occurred as described although the names – and in some cases relationships – of the characters have been changed. This book has come about through the prompting of many of my Syrian Christian friends who want people outside the Middle East to learn more about the life they had during those years.

The social problems prevalent in the Middle East today are featured, including inter-religious conflict between Christians and Moslems, sex, veiled women and security. However, the book aims mainly to describe daily life from a foreigner's viewpoint, based on my own personal experiences at that time.

Of course, the Syria that I knew has now disappeared under a religious and ideological conflict that has destroyed the country. It has been painful to write and realise that, for the most part, the places and the people described here no longer exist.

Syria lies on the 'fertile crescent', a swath of land in a rough boomerang shape running through Syria, Turkey and Iraq, that is recognised as the birthplace of agriculture and domesticated livestock. The world's first civilisations originated here; the world's earliest known written alphabet was created at Ugarit near the Syrian Mediterranean city of Lattakia.

The history of Syria and the countries around it is one of almost constant invasion, conflict and conquest, including civilisations such as the Egyptians, Assyrians, Hebrew Tribes, Seleucids, Babylonians, Byzantines, Hittites, Greeks, Romans, Saracens, Crusaders, Arameans, Amorites and Ottomans. Syria was a battleground during World Wars I and II and achieved independence at the end of the Second World War in 1946.

Syria's capital, Damascus, and its largest city, Aleppo, are the oldest continuously inhabited cities in the world, dating back around 3000 years. Judaism, Christianity and Islam were all born in this region and religion has continued to have a major influence on daily life at all levels of Syrian society.

Selemanieh

Selemanieh was a suburb at the centre of the Christian community in Aleppo. It was an unarguably middle- class suburb, and its residents were more settled than those in Midan, a suburb bordering Selemanieh on one side, and more friendly than those living in Azizieh, on another. It just touched a Moslem community: the most beautiful mosque in Aleppo, Jama' Al-Tawhid, rubbed shoulders with Saint George's Latin Church at the edge of Selemanieh. The principal roads through Selemanieh led travellers towards points further north and east: the Euphrates River towns of Raqqa and Deir-Ezzor, the Jezireh area north of the river, and also Turkey and Iraq (when the border was open). Given its prominent position at the crossroads of the city, Selemanieh has also experienced some of the heaviest fighting in Aleppo since 2010.

People living in Selemanieh were mostly Christian and from many denominations with a separate church for each one. These were to be found in scattered locations about the suburb, with larger ones such as the Greek Orthodox, the Armenian and the Latin churches occupying strategic sites on main roads. Other, more intimate churches stood all but hidden behind five and six story apartment blocks, or even nestled inside a group of buildings with nothing but a modest cross etched into the wall or wrought into an iron gate to signify their existence.

Selemanieh differed considerably from its neighbouring suburbs. Midan was mostly populated by Armenians, many of whom were early 20th century refugees into Syria, fleeing massacres in Turkey and who, by virtue of hard work, had been becoming upwardly mobile. However, Midan, the site of many of Aleppo's vehicle repair shops and other blue-collar industries, retained its lower-class facade, and a lot of the wealthier Armenians had moved on, many to Selemanieh.

Azizieh, on the other hand, was the home of the wealthy Christian families of Aleppo. Apartments no bigger than those that could be found in other Christian suburbs sold for two, three or more times the price. Azizieh was built during the 19th century and incorporated wide avenues and European-style apartment blocks and villas. Its shopping centre also featured boutiques, and prices in the most exclusive of them rivalled prices in Europe. In addition, residents in Azizieh had a reputation for being somewhat snobbish.

Selemanieh residents were anything but snobbish. At almost any time of the day or night you could, if you wished, find someone with whom to share a cup of coffee or tea. Selemanieh also boasted countless shops, many of them arranged in such a way as to include some seats for visitors, and all with coffee/tea-making facilities. The shops were mostly box-shaped, with one end opening out onto the street. Most of the time there were no back rooms and no exit from the rear, as the back wall generally buffeted against the wall of another shop on the street behind. Apartments generally occupied the floors above the shops and the buildings themselves were mostly made from concrete.

Except for the main thoroughfares, the streets in Selemanieh were quite narrow, with just room enough for two cars to pass, but on the relatively rare occasions that two cars did meet, they had to manoeuvre carefully. There were sidewalks, however these were almost inevitably filled with stalls and spill-over from the tiny shops (the proprietors displayed their goods outside as a temptation. It also gave them a reason to sit outside, with friends, and watch the passers-by) so that most people walked in the roads, a double hazard for negotiating vehicles, who must also take care not to bump the ever-increasing numbers of parked private cars.

There was also some light industry and much of this, for example cabinetmaking, took place outside - not only on the sidewalks, but in the middle of the road as well. It was certainly easier to walk around Selemanieh than to drive.

Almost any necessity could be purchased in Selemanieh. Shops abounded and itinerant traders also plied the streets with their wares, ranging from fruit and vegetables to inconceivable items created out of rainbow-coloured plastic. Many of these traders owned donkeys or horses and carts and their slow, stately movement around the streets added to the general road congestion. However, it made life remarkably easy. Several times a day the sound of a metal rod hitting gas bottles could be heard as a horse and cart, piled up with bottles of gas, ambled lazily along the streets. The sound carried to the top floors of every apartment, even in the winter when the windows were shut. One just had to run outside onto one's balcony, cry at the man, and he would replace your empty gas bottle. He would even carry it up into your apartment, charging a bit extra depending on the number of stairs he had to negotiate. Mazout, or diesel (for heating water and for stoves used for warmth in the winter) could be obtained in the same way, with the only main difference being that the vendor shouted 'mazout' at regular intervals as he negotiated the streets, rather than hitting his tank to attract custom. It was a bit harder on the lungs.

Except in the winter, when temperatures chased people indoors to huddle around their stoves, people sat mostly on their balconies, with or without visitors. It was a serious disadvantage not to have a balcony overlooking the street. You had to be able to watch your neighbours and, of course, be able to allow them to watch you. A well-placed balcony also allowed easy communication with people in the street below and friends could often tell at a glance if you were at home.

Families were not usually as large as in the Moslem communities: three children seemed to be about average, but a family of five still generated a large volume of washing. Women undertook this task most days and the resulting dripping lines of clothing leant out from the balconies over the streets. Hanging out the washing was an art form and women commented on their neighbours' techniques and judged their styles accordingly. Sheets had to be straight and the larger items should hide the more delicate and modest articles. It was also pleasing to the eye if the colours were coordinated.

Otherwise, balconies contained little decoration. Pot plants were rare, although plant life on balconies still existed in the form of drying vegetables. In the autumn, strings of aubergines and peppers decorated balconies like Christmas tree lights would come December. The vegetables were dried on the balconies for winter storage in anticipation of festive days when they would be reconstituted to their original size with water and then stuffed with meat and rice. Bunches of garlic and onions also graced the outside walls, as the dry air added shelf life to them.

The streets were narrow and their surfaces cracked, with countless depressions where water collected in pools on Fridays and when it rained. In fact, venturing outside on Fridays was more hazardous than during a thunderstorm. When it rained, which it only does during the winter and spring, you knew it was raining and could prepare accordingly by arming yourself with an umbrella. However, Friday was the main cleaning day. All the staircases in all the apartment blocks were hosed down, from top to bottom, in a simple and collective manner. Those living on the top floor would begin the job, working their way down to the next floor. As they finished, they announced the next person's turn by banging on their door. Those living on the first floor had the worst job: the stairs were necessarily dirtier through increased traffic and by the time all the water and gunge had reached them from the upper floors one could almost swim in the mire. Furthermore, they had the whole entrance to do. But they were compensated during the whole rest of the week: they had fewer stairs to climb.

As the bottom floors got swept out, all the water and muck would end up in the streets. Then, over the balconies from every floor would come a further volume of water as they were cleaned and swept out. For a pedestrian this was the most hazardous moment, as you not only had to watch where you placed your feet, side-stepping pools and rivulets of streaming grime, you also had to keep a look-out for cascades from above.

By the time I moved into Selemanieh the government had taken some major steps to improve the methods of rubbish disposal, so street cleaners passed daily, and piles of rubbish were already a thing of the past. During my first year in Aleppo, when I lived in another part of the city, rubbish used to pile up on many street corners, creating health hazards as well as horrific smells in the summer.

In fact, in Selemanieh we had only to put our rubbish outside our apartment door. For a fee of less than one American dollar a month, an elderly man climbed our stairs daily, collecting anything that we put out. The bags would generally be rummaged through for any recyclable items, with the rest destined for the rubbish tips outside the city.

I had not thought of living in Selemanieh. I lived in Shahaba during my first year in Aleppo, an upper-class (Moslem) suburb where most of the foreigners lived. The atmosphere there was completely different. The apartments were larger, more modern, and the streets were wider and cleaner. There were trees. At night one could hear silence, until the mosques broke it just before dawn. But Shahaba also seemed lifeless. Every building was separate to the next one, unlike the older parts of the city where the only separations between groups of buildings were the roads. Each building was quite large – normally three or four stories with one or two apartments on each floor. There were only a couple of shops scattered here and there, so you had to leave Shahaba to shop and for that you really needed a car. As most of the buildings had walled gardens or large verandas, most socialising took place behind walls and gates and there were fewer people in the streets.

In the end it was circumstances that pushed me to Selemanieh. I had come to Syria to undertake post-graduate research and enjoyed a reasonably generous grant during my first 18 months in the country. However, I returned to Syria after a break in Europe on a much-reduced budget, and in the meantime rents in Shahaba had skyrocketed. An apartment in Shahaba was now not only beyond my means, but I really needed to share with someone as well. At that time there were no other international students I knew needing accommodation, but one day a friend told me about a Syrian girl who was looking for an apartment and perhaps she would be willing to share. It was sheer providence. I wandered along to the girl's office and that was how I met Layla.

Layla

Layla was a rather unusual Syrian girl. The day I met her she was dressed in jeans and her thick, black, wiry hair was pulled about anyhow, without style or fashion. Make-up hardly touched her face, and her natural exuberance and unaffected laugh as we exchanged our first niceties were in stark contrast to the usual wariness accompanying typical inter-cultural introductions. In fact, she had an almost European air about her. In Europe she would be proclaimed attractive and her taste and style easily matched that of a European. I don't mean to say that she would not stand out in Syria. With just a little effort - which she made when she was going somewhere special - she could transform herself into a seemingly fashion-conscious, carefully made-up beauty. It was just that, unlike many Syrian girls, particularly Christians, she did not treat her everyday life - and certainly not the workplace - as a fashion parade.

However, the most unusual thing about her was that Layla, a young, attractive, unmarried Syrian girl, was not living at home with her parents. Few Syrians moved into apartments with friends as one does in Europe; most only left their parents' home when they married, and this applied particularly to women. Layla had come to Aleppo to attend university and her parents, being rather open-minded and modern in their thinking, had allowed her to remain in Aleppo after completing her degree in order to pursue a profession.

Layla was currently living in a rather conservative Moslem part of town and finding it difficult. Her female neighbours all covered themselves totally in black coats, gloves, face coverings and scarves when outside the confines of their homes and they did not hide their disapproval of a girl who not only wore skirts and jeans without the modesty of covering up her shapely legs with a coat, but worse still, kept her head uncovered. Like the Christian areas, Moslem suburbs also differed widely, with some being much more open than others. In the Christian areas, one seldom saw women with scarves covering their hair. Some Moslem districts had the same style, with girls wandering around in what Europeans would term 'normal dress' – trousers, skirts or dresses covering elbows and knees. Women living in other quarters would wear white or cream scarves over either normal dress, or perhaps a short trench coat. In stricter districts the dress code changed to black coats and scarves and finally, in some parts of town, nearly all the women would be totally covered in black, even to the extent of wearing black gloves. Their faces, too, would be totally covered by a black scarf without even the glimpse of an eye showing. It was in one of these most modest suburbs that Layla lived and she was desperate to move.

We began looking for an apartment. I was flexible as to what part of town we chose, but Layla prioritized Selemanieh as many of her friends were already located there. However, it was not easy to find a suitable place. Apartment after apartment fell by the wayside due to absolute grunginess, size, price or the problem of our being two single women, and one a foreigner. Furthermore, most Syrians did not rent apartments. They lived in their own places, which they generally purchased outright, there being no such thing as a mortgage available. Syrians were loath to rent an apartment to another Syrian, as the Law protected the tenant absolutely. Rents could not be raised, and tenants could not be asked to leave. There were some apartments that were rented for a couple of dollars a month, simply because the tenants had been in them for 20 years. Therefore, it was partly an advantage that I was a foreigner, as we were not protected by the same Law. Rents could go up and we could be kicked out.

However, the disadvantage was that I was young and single and, therefore, could potentially bring the building and the proprietor into disrepute. This attitude was brought home to me during one of our earlier apartment-hunting excursions. We had arranged to meet outside the Shahaba Sham, the city's five-star luxurious hotel near Layla's then current apartment. I had come straight from a game of squash dressed in a tracksuit that, while the trousers were tight-fitting, covered most of my body. I was also carrying my racket. One of the hotel guards came and told me to leave the area, accusing me of being a prostitute looking for clients.

We were looking for an apartment with at least three rooms: two bedrooms and a living room, and we did not want to pay more than 5000 Syrian pounds a month, which was equivalent to about 50 US dollars each at the open market exchange rate. (At the time, Syria had several exchange rates. The rate for foreigners having to pay for hotel accommodation was 11.2 Syrian pounds to the US dollar. International institutions had another rate of 23 for certain imported items. The official bank rate was 42, and the open market – or black market - rate fluctuated at around 50.)

One day I heard of an apartment belonging to the aunt of a work associate. It was in Selemanieh and had two bedrooms. It was on the second floor of a building on a quiet street and fronted a Church. The owners would be willing to provide whatever furniture we required.

Layla was busy at the time fixed for viewing the apartment, so I went with just a friend visiting from Europe. We were greeted by the woman, who was short, plump and dressed in a black mid-length dress, and her son - who spoke a little English - and they showed us around. It did not take very long. Two of the rooms were hardly larger than a cupboard; the kitchen resembled a galley on board a small yacht and someone fat or pregnant would never be able to close the bathroom door once inside. However, it had possibilities and we had become desperate. So, I smiled at the woman, said it was suitable, and asked about the price and the lease, which I wanted in Layla's name.

She did not answer immediately, rather she began talking to me about what sort of furniture she could provide and how it could all fit into the rooms. In the meantime, her son had taken my friend aside to request a favour from her: a letter of introduction so he could obtain a visa for Europe. My girlfriend felt trapped, as she did not want to destroy my chances of securing the apartment, so she murmured some non-committal response. Satisfied, the son turned around, smiling happily. He conversed quickly in Arabic with his mother and then turned to me.

'My mother wants you to think of us as your family. There is no problem at all, the apartment is yours. But the lease must be in your name. You will share with a Syrian girl, I think?'

I affirmed this, but said the lease had to be in Layla's name.

'This is not possible. The lease should be in your name, so that when you leave, she leaves. But it is no problem. As long as you are here, she can stay.'

I tried to insist on the lease being in her name, as it would make life easier for both of us. However, I knew it would be difficult and could be something to be negotiated later. Besides, we really needed an apartment. Layla had only a few days left to find another place to live as her apartment had already been signed over to someone else.

'What about the price?' I asked.

'Don't think about the price,' the son replied, smiling depreciatingly. 'We think of you as our family. We do not want to charge you very much. You are family, you are friends.' He smiled again, this time at my girlfriend, reminding her of her obligation to help him with his visa application.

'But what is the price?' I insisted.

'Nothing, really,' the son replied. 'If you just pay us 400 dollars it will be OK.'

I quickly calculated. Four hundred dollars was not a lot for a year, as the apartment was really worth about 600 dollars a year, so I decided that we should take it. While it was, in fact, illegal to pay the rent in dollars, I understood his reasons for wanting it in foreign currency and was willing to help him out in this manner. 'Four hundred dollars for one year,' I said. 'Of course, Layla cannot pay in dollars, but I can pay you the whole amount and she can pay me.'

'No, no,' the son said. 'Four hundred dollars a month.'

I gaped at him and burst out laughing. 'That is totally ridiculous. Good-bye.' I nodded to my girlfriend, 'let's go,' and we began to leave.

'Wait, wait, where are you going,' the son cried.

'You are being totally ridiculous. It is not even worth trying to negotiate with you. I know the prices here. What you are asking is more than what the most luxurious apartment in Shahaba commands. This is a tiny apartment, it is dingy, the kitchen has no amenities. We have other possibilities,' I added, lying. 'We are not desperate.'

'Wait.' He conferred with his mother, who began telling me in Arabic that I was like her daughter.

'OK,' he said. 'Two hundred dollars a month.'

'You are just being greedy. That is more than I earn. I have no desire to stay here a minute longer. Good-bye.'

He tried stopping us. He insisted. He said the price was good; he finally lowered it to 150 dollars a month. I was resolute. We inched our way out, agonisingly, fighting every step of the way. Once outside, while searching for a taxi, I launched into a tirade of unprintable language and we eventually consoled ourselves over huge ice creams at Sage's, a very pleasant up-market ice cream and cake parlour where, for 40 Syrian pounds, you could work your way through a chocolate-lover's delight worth at least 3000 calories.

The following day my colleague, who had directed me to the apartment, came to apologise and to tell me that his cousin would now be reasonable and accept the market price - and in Syrian pounds. Layla and I decided to keep it as a last resort. She had just found out from an old friend of hers that a fifth-floor apartment was free two doors away from him.

We move in

I DIDN'T GET TO SEE our apartment until Layla had it already signed and sealed. She didn't wax enthusiasm about it and certainly my first impression was somewhat clouded. We met on a Thursday evening so she could show me the apartment and introduce me to the landlord, Abu George. He was not yet aware that Layla planned to share with a foreigner and we were unsure how he would react.

There was a power cut at the time of our meeting. Power cuts were a normal - generally daily - occurrence throughout Syria, however it meant that I saw my future home for the first time by the light of a pen torch whose batteries were dying. It consisted of a sizeable front entrance, with the bathroom directly ahead. To the left of the entrance ran a corridor, with a large balcony running along one side and the toilet and kitchen along the other. There was one room - which became Layla's bedroom - at the end of the corridor. To the right of the entrance was a small, square room with no windows that was to be the living room. There were two rooms leading off this room. One was airless, dark and full of rotting furniture, while the other, entering through glass doors, was large and rectangular. It was, in fact, a balcony converted into a room with a chimney from the lower floors running up through the middle of it. However, throughout the apartment the walls and floors appeared grubby, the European toilet seat was broken, the Arabic toilet (a hole in the floor) smelled and the furniture was dusty and dirty. Several pieces were broken or in various stages of decay.

'I guess it can be cleaned up,' I commented at last.

We traipsed back down the 102 tiled and slightly cracked concrete stairs to the ground floor. I felt slightly dizzy from rounding the staircase the 10 necessary times while groping with two hands the dark, unfamiliar walls and banisters, the only light coming from an unseen moon and stars through large, open staircase windows. We then rushed through the dark streets at a quick trot, for Layla was already late for an appointment with friends, to Abu George's house. I followed her dazedly, watching out for cracks in the road, minding bags of rubbish, while Layla ran in front calling her uncertainty as to where she was heading. We backtracked two streets and tried a third, climbed a staircase to a third floor, descended again when she declared it to be the wrong house, and entered another doorway.

'I've only been here once,' she said, by way of explanation.

She finally settled on a suitable door and knocked. And knocked. And knocked. There was no answer, so we decided to leave the introductions for the following day.

I returned to the apartment at 10a.m. Friday morning, armed with detergent and cloths. We headed back to Abu George's house and knocked on the same door as the previous evening. A man answered this time, but it was not Abu George. 'Try the next floor up,' he said. I looked at Layla, and she laughed. 'Oh well, I'm not very good at directions and things.'

Abu George was a snake. At least that is how we named him outside his presence. Actually, we were more polite, we just likened him to a snake (Mitil Haiyah – literally, 'like a snake'). His moustache-less upper lip seemed permanently covered in a film of perspiration and his small beady eyes saw everything. However, during this first meeting he was very polite, and his wife served us coffee and Syrian chocolate sweets, followed by tea. At least he was honest and charged us only 5000 Syrian pounds ($100 US) a month for the apartment.

Layla already had a list of things she wanted done to the apartment, the most important being the transformation of the water heater from mazout (diesel) to electricity. At that time, the only way to have hot water was to light the heater in the bathroom, which ran on mazout. Being on the fifth floor, this would necessitate an almost constant running up and down with purchases of mazout. A fifth-floor apartment already posed some difficulties, as all the water had to be pumped up as well. When there was no electricity, we had no water either. Nor did we have water at night as it was cut off, but everyone in Aleppo on the town water supply had to put up with this inconvenience, at least during the summer months.

Abu George promised to take care of all our requests. In fact, it took him several weeks, so we found ourselves, in September when temperatures are still in the high 20's, without any water for several days. Both of us found alternative accommodation and we had to scrounge showers from friends for a fortnight. It was disconcerting, as Abu George would not turn up when he said he would and would arrive when no-one was home. Several times we arrived home to find him comfortably installed in our apartment, having used his own key to gain entry. He had no qualms about wandering around to check on our living arrangements and would often comment on how the furniture should be arranged.

After meeting with him, Layla and I set to work cleaning the apartment. Seeing it for the first time in the light of the day did not, at first, change my initial opinion of general dinginess. However, five hours and layers of dirt later, the walls turned into a bright cream, the furniture turned blue-mauve and a stone-work pattern became visible on the floors. Technically the apartment had five rooms plus a kitchen, a bathroom with a European toilet, a separate Arabic toilet and a spacious balcony. It was probably the balcony that kept the price down. It was not visible from the street and even an ostrich could not see the street from our apartment.

However, of the technical five rooms, one was useless as it had no access or light. We used this to junk the decrepit furniture, which was most of the stuff lying about. The apartment's previous occupants had been a group of male university students and they had obviously not been overly particular. Two of the rooms were connected, as there was no door between them - just the chimney. So practically speaking, the apartment was just three rooms, plus the large entrance hall. However, for our needs it was just about perfect.

There was a sixth-floor apartment above us which captured most of the heat, leaving the apartment quite cool. Being high up we caught breezes as we left all the windows open most of the year. At the time we took it we had no idea of its insulation in the winter months. However, by December we realised that the chimney, travelling up through our rooms, provided us with a novel form of central heating. We installed two stoves as well, but in the end, they were not used much.

I have never seen these types of stoves in Europe. A tank filled with mazout was placed upside-down over a pipe that led down into an opening at the bottom of the stove, and a valve on the tank permitted the mazout to drip or flow down the pipe. Once the fire was lit, the valve could be shut to allow just a slow drip drip drip of the mazout, at a rate of about two drips per second. The smoke escaped out through a chimney to the outside air. They were remarkably economical and provided a great deal of warmth in a small room. Food could even be heated on them. However, they were not terribly clean. Obviously, there were thousands of stoves around the city, all letting out their smoke during the winter months. Black specks of burned oil travelled on the breezes, slowly floating down to soil hanging washing or to land on your head as you walked.

Towards the end of that first day, I had made a trip back to my old accommodation and carted books and belongings to our new home. Layla and I celebrated the clean-up with tea before she headed off to her teaching job and I settled down to await the arrival of my first visitor.

Basel

Although a new resident to the Christian part of town, I already had a couple of friends there and one of them, Basel, had promised to drop in that first evening to celebrate my new home.

He arrived on time, an unusual characteristic for a Syrian, carrying some locally made ice cream, cake and a bottle of arak. Arak is a Middle Eastern alcohol made from grapes and tastes a lot like Greek ouzo. It is clear in colour, becoming cloudy with the addition of water. Most of the time Basel drank Raiyan, one of the numerous brand names of Syrian arak, and he had managed to instil in me a feeling of contempt for most of the other types of arak which to me, after Raiyan or Batta (another brand), tasted rather like turpentine. However, I had developed a taste for Raiyan and drank it diluted by about 50 per cent with water and ice.

We drank the arak, ate the ice cream and cake and Basel then took me out for a walk around my new district. He pointed out all the best shops to me; shops where I could purchase hummus (a dip made from chickpeas), fool (a fava bean breakfast), khubz (bread), grilled chickens, yoghurt and milk, olives, oil, vegetables, fruit, eggs, meat, toilet paper and alcohol. Each tiny shop specialised in a small number of items and shopping could take a long time. We passed two supermarkets and wandered into one (most shops stayed open until nine or ten o'clock at night). The supermarket shelves were stacked with a selection of tinned goods and plastic bags filled with flour, sugar, tea and lentils. There were some shelves with Kleenex and washing powders. An open fridge displayed Syrian Gouda cheese and cows' milk yoghurt. There were a couple of packets of dubious-looking luncheon meat and some tins of condensed milk. Near the one check-out counter were three shelves of Syrian-made alcohols, ranging from a local cherry brandy to gin and wines. There were about 10 different varieties of arak. In another corner were shampoos, conditioners and hair sprays lounging near a selection of toothpastes and a rainbow of toothbrushes.

Down on the main road we passed several jewellers, their windows bulging with gold trinkets and chains. There were also some nut and seed stalls, their owners sitting on stools on the sidewalk, absent-mindedly munching on sunflower seeds and throwing the cases out into the street.

Further along the street was an outdoor café divided into two sections: one for men and the other reserved for families. We entered the second part and sat at a table next to a small pool with a little fountain in the middle, which idly threw out a tiny jet of water. A cat jumped onto the edge of the pool and lent over to take a drink, her tail darting about in the air behind her. Along the edges of the café grew some green plants and they helped dapple the light from strings of light bulbs, creating an intimate atmosphere. The chairs, however, were plastic and rickety and the tables were covered with plastic as well. A jug of water and one glass graced the table, as water glasses were generally shared in cafés. We ordered coffee and a tea.

'This is the first time that I've sat in the family section of this café,' said Basel, looking about him.

I looked at him in surprise. He was in his mid-30s, intelligent, attractive and certainly personable. But he had not yet married and despite being Christian, it was not really normal to spend an evening alone with a girl that you were not related to. We had already been out to dinner a couple of times on our own, but normally people dined in groups and often the groups were just of men. Most of the best restaurants in Aleppo were situated at the edge of Selemanieh: there were about 10 lining a dual carriageway with flying saucer-like multi-coloured lights decorating the grassed median strip. In fact, the median strip covered the Quake River, a dirty stream running under the city and along which, outside the city limits, irrigated vegetables grew (fertilised by sewage from Aleppo). A couple of the restaurants catered for family groups, but most of them had only men as their clientele. This did not mean that women could not enter, however they did not usually do so.

After walking home again, I made my way alone up the five flights of stairs to our apartment, while music from a tape cassette shop on the corner of our building blared up after me. An argument could be heard through the thin veneer of the apartment walls. I undressed and slipped into bed but could not sleep. It was nearly 11p.m. and noise was loud around me.

The music ceased for a brief respite while the tape was changed. Either the owner or a client evidently preferred a male vocalist to Fairuz, the famous Lebanese singer. I lay and listened to the beat, which was already familiar to me, and despite my tiredness found myself mouthing, quietly, the words to the song, Wa-la marra, which cries a man's sorrows for having never had the chance of dancing with the woman he loves.

Most Arabic music runs along the same theme, in fact, that of unrequited love. So few of their favourite songs end happily, that it seems hardly surprising that Arabs have such a fatalistic attitude towards life and love.

As the song ended the cassette shop shut and so did my eyes. My first sleep in Selemanieh had arrived.

You can't sleep

AN HOUR LATER MY EYES were jerked rudely open. Someone was frantically beating a drum right beside my bed. I started up in horror: after all, I hardly knew Layla, what was she doing? What could she be thinking? As my eyes and ears adjusted themselves to my surroundings, I realised that the drum was actually outside the window... but we were five stories up! I craned my neck outside to see, on a balcony on the floor below, a group of people starting an impromptu party complete with drum, tambourine, stamping feet and loud chanting. Glancing at my watch, I realised that it was nearly 1a.m. Swiss regulations prohibiting any form of noise after 10p.m. flickered through my mind as I turned on the light to search for some earplugs.

Of course, they were not a lot of help as some noises just cannot be shut out. Moreover, the stamping feet were actually vibrating the building - or at least my bedroom floor, situated as it was directly above the party. I finally removed the plugs at 2.37a.m. and settled back to sleep.

At 3a.m. I was woken again. Prayer call. Again, my mind began its thought process: but I live in Selemanieh. This is a Christian neighbourhood; how can I hear mosques? I use the word in its plural form deliberately because I could distinguish at least four different calls, albeit quite distant. Fortunately, I have always loved the sound of the prayer call, so it was not difficult to lie in bed listening to the chanting and, in fact, thanking Allah (God) that there were some mosques within hearing distance of the house. The sound of the mosques also meant that the streets outside were now quiet!

Although normally an early riser - I'm usually awake if not out of bed by 6a.m. - I do like eight hours of sleep each night. As the mosques returned to sleep at around 3.30a.m., I really needed to sleep until about 9.30a.m. to catch my quota. However, experience had already shown me that Arabs in general do not care much for lying in, so I was not really surprised to be woken up, once again, just after 7a.m. However, I was not prepared for its method, which consisted of a steadily rising crescendo of shouting and laughing children as buses disgorged their loads into a school situated directly across the street. It was not a normal school by my standards either. Its playing grounds were not attached to the ground at all, but rather perched on the fourth floor, on top of many of the classrooms. In other words, the screaming children were directly across from my bedroom window. With my glasses on, I could count the buttons on their shirts as they chased each other around the yard.

Right on 7.30a.m., a bell rang and all noise ceased. A man's voice then rang out, followed by a collective chant, proclaiming the greatness of the United Arab State (Syria, Lebanon, Jordan and Palestine) and undying love, esteem and respect for the great leader, Hafez Al-Assad (Syria's then President). This was followed by a patriotic song. Then the crescendo of children's chatter began again.

Sleep now being useless, I got up and headed for the bathroom. The shower was cold as Abu George had not yet begun work on its transformation onto the electrical circuit. However, while it was now September and only 8a.m., temperatures were still high enough that the cold shower was not too tortuous. The shower itself was a simple pipe running up the wall, opening out into a fairly low-pressured spray directed straight down from the ceiling. The water ran straight onto the floor, which sloped towards a drain near the back of the European toilet. In one corner stood a plastic scraper which was used to push the water towards the drain at the completion of the shower. The floor tended to dry remarkably quickly, and the system kept the bathroom floor extremely clean.

For breakfast there was only a bit of cake left over from the previous evening, so I decided to head out and do some shopping. Layla was still asleep - it seemed that she was used to the noise of the school children - so I went out to explore on my own.

Shopping

At the bottom of the five flights of stairs was a cake shop. As I emerged into the sunlight from the dim staircase I almost bumped into its owner, a short middle-aged man with black hair and a thick moustache. He was sweeping the sidewalk outside his shop window, where mouth-watering cakes and cookies were lined up like soldiers on oven trays. Most of the cakes – full sized ones and individual slices – were decoratively iced in garish green, yellow and pink. The cookies were a variety of shapes, mostly baked with pistachios. On the other side of the road were three young men sitting on stools drinking coffee. Half-completed cabinets jutted out into the road around them, so I deduced they were having a break from work. The baker smiled at me and stopped sweeping. As I turned the corner by the tape shop, once again blaring out the top of the Arab charts, I caught a glimpse of the baker striking up a conversation with the cabinetmakers. They were all looking at me, so I figured that I was the topic of their conversation.

On the next street corner were several villagers selling small quantities of fruit and vegetables. 'Villagers' was the stock name used to denote country people undertaking farming for a living. While the men could be difficult to spot as they, like many other working-class Syrians, Christians and Moslems alike, dressed in jalabiyas (long, cotton gowns) and checked scarves, the women were easily distinguishable. Unless they were in mourning (when they dressed in black), their dresses were always brightly patterned and colourful, with their head scarves loosely knotted at the neck. Often their chins and the backs of their hands would be tattooed with wavy patterns of dark green henna and a glimpse of escaped locks of hair sometimes revealed overuse of red henna to dye their long tresses. Sometimes some of their teeth were capped with gold, a form of decoration similar to earrings, as the caps could be taken out at night.

Groups of men and women were crowded around the villagers, requesting quantities of fruit. Scales were used to weigh the purchases, with the weights being different sized stones. I selected half a dozen tomatoes and some cucumbers and a gnarled-handed woman crouching on the ground took them from me to check against her stones. As the scales dipped, she added another vegetable to them and, glancing up at me with a lined face aged anything from 25 to 75, quoted a total price of 25 pounds.

Further up the street two horse-drawn carts completely blocked the street while their owners haggled with local residents over the prices of bananas (an imported good) and melons, for which the end of the season was near. I turned into a little fruit and vegetable stall to buy some apples and the thin and slightly vacant-eyed owner weighed out two kilos for me.

I crossed the road to the bakery where a crowd of people - mostly young boys - were pushing, waving bills of money in the air. Between the crowd and the road were two long black metal tables on which people were laying out their loaves of bread to cool and dry. Due to lack of space, others were laying the bread out over the sidewalk. Those with their purchases were pushing their way out of the throng of people, the hot, round, flat loaves flopping over their hands. Each loaf, called Syrian two-layered bread, was about 25 centimetres in diameter with a thickness of about half a centimetre.

I shoved my way into the crowd around the bakery and, eventually nearing the front, could see the baking process. At the back two men were preparing the rounds from a huge tub of dough and throwing them onto a conveyor belt that disappeared into the depths of the oven. A few seconds later the loaves emerged, cooked, with hot air lifting the upper portion of the loaf into the air. They were collected by two more men and either counted or weighed, then handed over to the customers. Approximately five rounds weighed one kilogram and cost five Syrian pounds (10 US cents).

People wanting more than five rounds had the bread weighed, with the loaves getting torn in half in order to reach the correct weight. If you wanted a bag to put the bread in, one round was taken off the total weight of the bread. I proffered my five pounds and juggled the five steaming loaves back out of the crowd. Then I laid them at the edge of one of the tables to allow them to cool enough to get them into a bag.

My next stop was the supermarket where, using a little basket such as in a European supermarket (trolleys were unheard of), I collected some flour, sugar, eggs, salt, spices and, feeling homesick, half a kilogram of Anchor New Zealand butter (I grew up in New Zealand). In fact, normally there were only two types of butter available, both unsalted. A Danish variety was the one more frequently to be found.

At the checkout counter (there was only one), a man totted up the amounts on an electric till while another, visibly the first one's elderly father, carefully placed the goods in a large black plastic bag, adding a couple of wrapped sweets that were sitting in a bowl at the end of the counter. Maintaining his seat on an old stool, he handed me the bag while I struggled to put my wallet back into my purse.

I staggered back towards the apartment, passing a couple of clothing shops and a window full of soft cuddly toys. However, Selemanieh didn't really have many shops other than for food.

In Aleppo there were two main areas that women went shopping for clothes: Azizieh and Telal. Telal was situated not far from the old souk in Aleppo and was Moslem. It had a carless street which made it wonderful for wandering around. However, the fashion of the clothes was generally quite modest yet 'over the top'. Bobbles and sequins abounded, along with ribbons, lace and bright colours. The sleeves were generally long, as were the skirts. Azizieh, being the upper-class Christian suburb, boasted higher prices, with the clothes and shoes being sometimes really beautiful. In addition, with careful shopping and determined bargaining, items could be obtained at reasonable prices.

Christians in general hated bargaining, unlike Moslems who usually treated it as a game. Most items in the Christian shopping areas had a fixed price; unlike the souk, which was Moslem. However, you could bargain in Azizieh. You would already have a starting point in the indicated price, but this was easily lowered, generally by around 10 or 15 per cent. I adopted two techniques for bargaining, and both seemed to achieve the same result. If the man asked for, say, 600 pounds, I would counter-offer with either 400 or 500 pounds, depending on whether I thought he would counter-offer yet again. The final price would be 500 pounds.

A better technique was to force the shop keeper into thinking he was being generous. It made payment easier, especially when he had to give you some change. In the first technique, he might have felt that you had got one over him. This was bad for his ego, especially as I was, at the same time, both a foreigner and a woman. He might try to short-change me. So, technique number two was wonderful, and worked in most cases.

You select the item that you wish to buy. Holding it in your hand, you ask the price, even if it is written on the article.

'Idesh?' (How much).

'Siteh milleh' (six hundred).

You look questioningly at the article, and ask, hesitatingly, as if you can't quite believe it, 'Siteh milleh?' And nine times out of ten, the man would reply,

'Oh alright, five hundred.' You smile sweetly, he replies in kind and you become good friends. Of course, in the unlikely event that he simply says to you, 'yes, six hundred,' then you could adopt technique number one. But the atmosphere would be less friendly.

This worked in the souk as well. One day I was in the souk with some other foreigners and wanted to purchase an Iranian tablecloth.

The usual price was 1500 pounds, and I knew several people who had bought them with the price always sticking at 1500 pounds, no matter what the starting price. The people I was with were looking at carpets, so when I chose the tablecloth, the shop keeper, Mohammed, told me the price was 1500 pounds. He put it aside for me so I could pay just before we left.

After the usual sumptuous display of carpets, during which time my companions purchased nothing, we made to leave. I reminded Mohammed about the tablecloth. 'Oh yes,' he said, retrieving it.

'Fifteen hundred pounds, you said?' I questioned, looking him in the eyes.

'Oh, make it 1300,' he said.

'Thirteen hundred?' I still held the element of doubt in my voice.

'Twelve hundred, then,' he said, smiling. I had intended to pay 1500 pounds all along, so I wasn't even really bargaining. Yet he, happily, dropped the price by 20 per cent.

Promenades

By the time my first weekend in Selemanieh was over - for us the weekends were Fridays and Saturdays - I had settled into the apartment. The volume of noise at night did not decrease, although fortunately the impromptu parties from our neighbours downstairs were not an everyday occurrence. I also found that after a week or so, I could sleep through the music shop and the mosques. The school always defeated me, however most days I was up before that noise began.

Being a Christian suburb, most shops were open on Fridays, the only exceptions being those run by a handful of Moslems who religiously took each Friday off. On the other hand, only a few shops were open on Sundays. Weekends in Syria could sometimes be confusing. Most companies, the government included, took just one day off, usually the Friday, observing this day as the weekend. However, Christian companies, industries, shops and schools operated on Fridays and kept Sundays for their weekly break. Most people worked Saturdays. ICARDA, the International Centre for Agricultural Research in Dry Areas, where I worked, retained the tradition of an international (westernized) centre and had a five-day working week. However, it deferred to the Moslem community by working from Sunday to Thursday, leaving Fridays and Saturdays as the weekend.

So, on Sundays we would not have the inconvenience of the morning wake-up call from the school, as it was a Christian one. But I had to work, so did not benefit at all by it. However, on a late Sunday afternoon, returning to Selemanieh was almost like arriving at a peaceful haven. Only some food shops were open, and the streets were calm and silent except for handfuls of children playing soccer. People were resting, awaiting the fall of darkness (never very late, even in summer) for their weekly promenade.

Sunday evening was the time for Christian families to undertake their weekly sortie. By 8p.m. the streets would be full of people, all dressed up in their best clothes. Girls and young women sported almost outrageous hairstyles, held up on top of their heads at seemingly impossible angles by huge quantities of spray, pins and ribbons. Most of the time their hair - of any colour, black was not unique - was long and thick, and often it was, naturally or with human aid, curly or wavy. They were quite fashion-conscious as well, although by European standards the dress was perhaps a little over-done, with masses of bobbles, dazzling bits of lace and ribbon, huge ornamental buttons, ruffles and sequins all competing for attention on brightly coloured skirts and blouses or dresses. High heels were a necessity, as was a certain weight of jewellery and make-up.

Skirts could be of almost any length, and there were no real restrictions on how much of your shoulders and neck might be revealed. During my first year in Syria, living in a Moslem district, I was always careful never to wear - in the streets - skirts above the knee or really short-sleeved shirts. In fact, in European style I generally hung around in jeans. However, peer or neighbourhood pressure in Selemanieh completely changed my style of dress. I never went for the sequins and bobbles, but I began wearing skirts 90 per cent of the time and never worried too much about length. If I was going out to a party in the evening, Layla would often push some of her clothes onto me, as they were considerably more stylish than anything I had. For the first time in my life I began receiving compliments for my dress. That, of course, did not encourage me to return to jeans! I noticed my style getting more and more daring - or Syrian - as my year in Selemanieh wore on.

The Sunday evening promenades were not exclusively for women: it often seemed that the whole Christian population was out in the streets, particularly when the weather was fine, profiting from their evening off. Girls and unmarried women tended to walk together, arm-in-arm, while their opposites - young men - also banded together, often in groups of three or four. Then there were the families: young married couples pushing a stroller and either leading an older sibling by the hand or carrying her/him. Older women, often dressed in black, completed the picture as they, too, headed outside to walk together. The only sector of the population visibly missing in this weekly stroll was that of the older men. A quick glance inside one of the many coffee houses along the route cleared up that mystery. Large groups of men would be huddled around nargilehs - water pipes - and backgammon boards, all drinking gallons of tea and/or coffee and all smoking cigarettes. Frequenting a coffee house was not a pastime for any one particular group in Aleppo as it seemed that, proportionately-speaking, Christian men enjoyed them as much as the Moslems.

As the evening wore on, the streets would gradually disgorge of their masses and the restaurants would begin to fill up in their place. Sunday evening was really the time when large mixed groups could be seen enjoying each other's company. At other times the tables were almost always filled with men. However, some of the more popular restaurants had begun setting aside 'family' areas, where only groups including women could sit. One restaurant in particular, Wanas, catered almost exclusively for family groups to the extent that men-only groups of diners were actively refused admittance, particularly in the summer, although they could sit outside - on one part of the terrace only.

Wanas produced the best food of all the restaurants in Aleppo, which tended to be fairly similar wherever you ate, but it was also the most expensive place (not taking into consideration the three 'international' hotels - the Shahaba Sham, the Amir Palace and the Pullman - although you really only frequented these three hotels for European food). Being on a limited budget but enjoying restaurant food necessitated a search for a cheaper place. I was finally introduced to a lovely little restaurant near Wanas, called Babel. Although informed that the only women who ever went inside were reputed to be prostitutes, I began going there frequently; sometimes in a group from work and sometimes with just one or two friends. The owner and his staff began to get to know me and we always got excellent service, even when I went with only a girlfriend. The excellent service generally included free dessert in the form of a platter of fruit.

Layla enjoyed the food there as well. However, as it was not considered a decent restaurant for a Syrian girl to frequent, she always posed as a foreigner, leaving me to do the ordering. One evening, when I deferred to her in a choice of dishes, she answered in Arabic without thinking.

'My!' Exclaimed the waiter, a large, chubby man, dressed in a tuxedo, with slicked back hair and a greased moustache, who was perpetually combing his hair when he wasn't taking orders or serving Arak, 'My, you do speak good Arabic!'

Friends of mine - regulars at Babel - were not really sure of my going there alone with just a girlfriend, but two things confirmed our total acceptance at Babel, despite the exclusive male clientele around us. The dishes served to us always seemed a little larger and a little more lavishly decorated than those on other tables, and the bill - which our slicked-up waiter brought to us on a small piece of paper half covered by a cloth, written especially for us in the numerical form used in Europe, rather than the way numbers were represented in Syria - was always incredibly cheap. With just a girlfriend or two, and almost no matter what we ate or drank, the price always seemed to be 200 pounds. This amounted to two US dollars each and represented roughly half the price that we paid when accompanied by men.

One Sunday evening Layla and I fought our way through the fashion parade of strollers along the Selemanieh High Street for a quiet meal at Babel. As we approached the restaurant, we saw a donkey standing unconcernedly outside in the middle of the road. He had neither halter nor harness but seemed loath to move. As he happened to have chosen a busy T-junction at which to repose himself, traffic skirted around him, headlights flashing and horns blaring. He would not move. Layla, being a typical Syrian girl in some respects in that she feared all animals, hid behind me, shaking, as we crossed the street, even though the donkey was some 30 metres away. However, she would walk 100 metres to avoid passing a cat as well.

As it was the middle of Ramadan, the restaurant was empty and the entire staff - two waiters and some five servers and kitchen staff, plus the restaurant owner - were gathered around a television in one corner of the room. We were seated at the best table in the house and we began our usual play on languages. Layla, pretending to be European, refused to have anything to do with the ordering of the food and refused to speak Arabic. This was in direct contrast to the usual scene at home, where it was practically forbidden to speak English. Often, I would not understand Layla, but she would persist by repeating herself and repeating herself in Arabic. It was frustrating at times, but I am, of course, deeply grateful to her, because she forced me to learn Arabic. It would have been much easier for her to use English all the time, at which she was proficient.

However, I was always able to get my own back at Babel. I would persist in speaking Arabic, and she would persist in replying in English. Our conversations went something like this:

'Marhaba (hello)'. This is from me to the waiter. He stands poised, bits of scrappy paper and a pen at the ready, and asks what we would like.

'Shu biddek (what would you like)?' I ask Layla.

'What would I like?' She asks, slowly, as if trying to understand my words. 'Whatever you like. You order.'

'Biddek Arak?' I ask.

'Arak? Are you going to drink Arak'?

'Ashrub Arak (I'm taking Arak).'

'If you are going to drink Arak, I will have some with you, otherwise I'll have a cola,' replies Layla, pretending to misunderstand me. I turn to the waiter, who has been desperately trying to follow our conversation.

'Wahid Arak, Min Fadlak. Raiyan. (Raiyan Arak, please)'. I turn back to Layla.

'Wa akol. Shu biddek (what food would you like)?'

'The usual. You decide.'

'Biddek creme toum (creamed garlic) wa moutabbal (an eggplant dip)?'

'Whatever.'

The waiter then charges in. He's begun to understand the conversation, his ears pricked for words like creme toum, which he knows we always order anyway.

'Batata? Salata?' He asks.

'La (no). Creme toum, moutabbal, hummus, um.. muhammara (a roasted red pepper dip).' I turn back to Layla. 'Biddek muhammara? or dibsflehfleh (another sort of red pepper dip, rather hotter)?'

'What is dibsflehfleh?' She asks, round-eyed in innocence.

I give up and tell the waiter muhammara.

'What about those cheese things?' Layla asks suddenly.

'Which ones?' I reply, forgetting my Arabic for a second.

'You know, the ones shaped like this.' She makes a movement with her hand.

'Kibbeh?' The waiter asks, trying to understand her gestures. But kibbeh is not cheese based.

'What is their name?' I persist.

'You know what I mean,' she replies, refusing to divulge her knowledge of Arabic food. By this stage we are both laughing, so I put the waiter out of his misery and order borak (a sort of cheese spring roll) and some toshka (meat and cheese cooked together inside two slices of Arabic bread) which we both love.

Our poor slick waiter could never make head or tail of our conversations in front of him, until the famous evening when he caught Layla saying something in Arabic and complimented her for it. The next time we went together, I got stuck in my description of something new we wanted, and the waiter turned to Layla for help. Quick as a flash, I said 'La, ma-tifham:' (no, she doesn't understand). He spent the rest of the evening sighing and grovelling like David Copperfield's Uriah Heep, spitting out at Layla at regular intervals, 'Qua-a-is, Mademoiselle?' (is everything alright?). When we finally left Layla followed my quiet 'Shukran kiteer, Ma'asalama' (Thank you very much, goodbye) with a loud wave and 'Thanks a lot!' with a cheeky smile. The following evening Basel told the waiter that Layla was from Spain.

That Sunday evening in Ramadan we were only joined by one other couple, a man with a woman wearing a scarf on her head. However, they ate and left quickly, so most of the time we had the full attention of all the staff, that is when they were not otherwise engaged in watching television, which was much more interesting. The slick waiter did not seem to be enjoying the soccer game much. He spent nearly all the time in front of a mirror ornamenting one wall, his comb in one hand. From our window seat we could spot Wanas across the road, bursting with customers simply because it was an Armenian restaurant and because it was Sunday. Things were quieter in Babel and the food was just about as good. Besides, Layla would have ordered at Wanas, and in Arabic. It would not have been so much fun.

By the time we walked home it had started to rain and the streets were deserted. The promenades were over for another week.

In fact, it took a trip to Mahardeh, a village about three hours southwest of Aleppo, for me to fully understand the logic behind these Sunday evening promenades. Layla's family was from Mahardeh, whose population is 100 per cent Christian. Probably its greatest claim to fame now is that Syria's only Olympic gold medallist came from Mahardeh. In fact, she was a school mate of Layla. Her name was Ghada Shouaa and she competed in the 1992 Barcelona Olympics, coming 25th. Layla was very proud of her.

In 1995, Ghada became the world champion in the heptathlon and at Atlanta in 1996 she won the Olympic Gold.

The first time I visited Mahardeh it was wintertime. However, the Sunday evening promenades had become an institution there, so they still took place. Another friend of Layla's had dubbed the promenade the cattle market, but I changed the name to 'souk al-banat', literally the 'market of women'. By 6.30p.m. one particular street in Mahardeh would become lined with young men and their motorcycles or motor scooters, and they would lean nonchalantly against the sides of the buildings, or sit on their parked cycles, chatting to each other while groups of young women, dressed even more stunningly than in Aleppo, walked up and down the road. Sometimes they would be followed or joined by some of the young men. They would walk up to the end of the road, turn and walk down again, turn and walk back up. If walking became boring, one could repair to one of the cafes along the road for a drink.

At one stage we caught sight of two young men and two young women who had seemingly got cut off from the rest of the crowd. 'Ah,' I said, 'They have made their purchases.' I was told that this was the way people met and marriages were arranged. It seemed incredible in a small town where everyone knew each other and where most were related anyway. Returning to Aleppo, the logic of the Sunday evening strolls became very clear, as did the need to look your best.

Nabil

One of the first people I met in Selemanieh was a bookshop owner called Nabil. I was introduced to him during my first week in Selemanieh by Basel, who was a close friend, with the words, 'if there is ever anything you need, Nabil can help, seriously.' Such promises were frequent in Syria and had to be taken lightly, hence the addition of the word 'seriously' to the offer. How many times did I meet someone who, after a five-minute conversation, would offer to help me 'whenever I needed it?' I wondered how any of them would react if I did turn up on their doorstep one night seeking their aid.

This propensity to make empty offers is quite Arab. One person at ICARDA used to sit down in the canteen and immediately say 'tfadl' (help yourself) while airily waving his hand over his plate of food. As everyone else at the table already had their own lunches, the gesture was totally ridiculous and he was frequently told this. However, he persisted in this ritual politeness until one day two friends of his took him at his word and cleaned his whole plate. He never said 'tfadl' in the canteen again.

Nabil's offer was not empty, and he quickly became a close friend. In the year I lived in Selemanieh, I only ever once saw him actually pocket any money, and it was some 30 Syrian pounds (60 US cents) for photocopying. More often than not, I saw him either making coffee, pouring coffee, drinking coffee or clearing up coffee. At one stage, when Nabil decided to embark on a health campaign, he cut down on the coffee and offered only tea. This period was short-lived. I think the major problem was that the campaign also involved giving up cigarettes and he was normally a two packet a day smoker.

Nabil, like many Christian Syrians in his social category, was in his mid-30s and was single. Such a situation always remained a complete enigma to me as he was extremely kind, very personable and quite attractive, although he recognised that the loss of 10 kilograms would not go amiss. He used to joke all the time about the girl he would one day marry. He would vividly describe her to me and, in the next breath, ask me how Layla or another of my girlfriends was. One eye was always kept on the pedestrian circulation outside and, as part of his act, he would always raise his eyebrows and laugh in my direction when a young and shapely woman passed.

His shop was always crowded - with people rather than books, although I finally managed to persuade him to fill his empty shelves - so his constant running to and from the back room, where his gas burner was kept, with coffee was understandable. He also kept a backgammon board, with which he played constantly. However, he never offered to play me.

One evening when I arrived, he was in the middle of a game with a man we jokingly referred to as 'The Sheikh', even though he was neither Bedouin nor a tribal leader (which is what a 'Sheikh' normally is). The Sheikh was always well-dressed in a suit and tie and in the winter sported a fashionable coat. His salt and pepper hair and huge moustache were thick and well-groomed, and he was tall and imposing, giving an air of authority commanding respect. Nabil ceded his place to me.

'But can she play?' The Sheikh asked, looking at me slightly disdainfully. After all, I was a woman and only admitted into this sanctuary of male society because I was an ajinabieh (a foreigner).

'Of course,' Nabil replied, going outside to discuss business with a passer-by.

The Sheikh and I settled down to play. Nabil had left himself in a rather poor position and I was unable to improve on it before the end of the game. We set the counters up for a second round.

Whether it was luck or skill - I have played backgammon for years - I won this game. The Sheikh threw in the towel while I still had five counters to remove, and he immediately got up and walked out of the shop. I was left alone. After about five minutes, I understood that he was not coming back to play another game, despite the fact that one would normally sit and play some 10 or more games in a row. I put the board away and my victory was never ever mentioned. The Sheikh was so ashamed at having been beaten by a woman and an ajinabieh, that it would not have done even for Nabil to tease him about it.

Besides the constant supply of coffee, Nabil also became my self-appointed Arabic teacher. His command of the English language was largely confined to 'OK, see you,' followed by a hysterical giggle and a wringing of his hands. We were, therefore, forced to communicate in Arabic and Nabil was wonderful in that he had the patience and the will to understand my rendition of his language and to formulate simple sentences in return. Over the months, although we were not often alone in the shop, we managed to discuss at length any number of subjects, ranging from women and marriage to differences in life in other countries, American and British politics concerning the Middle East, agriculture and industry.

However, these conversations took place in the future. They were a far cry from my first lesson with him, which occurred on Friday lunchtime some three weeks after I had met him. I was passing his shop and he called me in, offering me the inevitable cup of coffee.

As we drank our coffee he was, as was his habit, doodling on some scraps of paper. Most of the time he made elaborate scripts of words and names - in Arabic - and I started to read them. He stopped the elaborate drawings and began to write quick, individual words in order to test me, such as car, tree, man, girl, house, Australia, Canada, Syria, New Zealand and the United States.

'America,' he said, laughing and pointing to the last word. 'America, the best!'

I made a face, largely because he expected me to. His parents were just in the process of obtaining green cards and he hoped to be able to immigrate to the United States. I constantly told him that New Zealand was better, while he dared label my beloved country a mere off-shoot of Australia. Small objects frequently flew, as missiles, in Nabil's shop.

So far so good in the test. I had managed to read, and understand, all the words. Then he began to look around him for inspiration: book, office, pen, paper; and then to the street outside, road, sun, lemons, onions, tomatoes (there was a fruit and vegetable stall across the road). From there I began to get stuck and Nabil started trying to explain the meaning of the words to me.

'It is like, heck, and heck,' he would say, pulling his fingers around an imaginary elongated ball, 'and it is sort of black.' He would pretend to chop and eat it.

'Ah,' I would exclaim, 'eggplant.' And we would go onto the next word.

One day Nabil needed some help at work and I volunteered. In compensation he invited Basel and me to dinner at Wanas. Before going, he insisted that the only things he would order would be Arak and creme toum. He was a devotee of these two items and considered he had found a kindred spirit in me. In the event, we ended up with a feast of dishes.

A few weeks later I popped in briefly in the morning on my way out. I had no time for coffee, so Nabil elicited a promise from me to pass again in the evening. However, by the time evening came I was shattered. Layla was cooking dinner and asked if I wanted some. She had guests.

'Give me half an hour,' I said. 'I promised to pop in and see Nabil, so I guess I should.' I dragged myself into jeans and a jumper and stumbled down the 102 stairs and the road around to his shop. I walked in to find it curiously almost empty. There was just Nabil and one of his friends who was, unusually, married.

'Ah, there you are,' Nabil cried, 'we've been waiting for you. We're going out to dinner.'

I protested. I was tired, I wasn't dressed, Layla was cooking. However, they dismissed all arguments and bundled me into a waiting car. We headed for Wanas, where tuxedoed waiters offered excellent service, and entertainers in the same standard of dress would, late in the evening, begin the nightly entertainment of music and a selection of Arabic, Armenian and French songs.

Unlike Babel, which was a rather small restaurant, Wanas could seat over 200 people inside at a time. Its outside seating in the summer could double its clientele. It was an elegant restaurant: an aging gentleman sat by the door to hang coats and scarves up behind huge sliding mirrored doors. The tables were all covered in two cloths, white and teal blue linen, and the teal blue napkins were freshly laundered. Waiters and servers lined the walls. The waiters took the orders and the money, and the servers brought the food, wheeling it around the restaurant on large trolleys. While its menu included a selection of European food, its Arabic, or Armenian, food was excellent and generally rated the best in Aleppo. As some people considered Aleppo the final word in good Arabic cuisine, one could suggest that Wanas was the best Arabic restaurant in the world.

Once there, Nabil ordered an enormous quantity of food and Arak. His friend could speak a little French, so we stumbled along in a sort of mixture of French and Arabic for about two hours, when the friend had to leave, as his wife expected him home. Nabil and I remained behind, and he ordered some fruit to wash down the meal, as well as some more Arak. We began telling jokes.

Most of Nabil's jokes were of the Irish type. Syrians tended to pick on people from Homs, an industrial town about half way between Damascus and Aleppo. The dunce in the jokes was always the man from Homs and I was able to laugh at all his jokes despite my ineptness at the language, largely because the few words I understood helped me to picture the joke as an English person would talk about the Irish. His jokes ran along the lines of 'how do you burn the ear of a man from Homs? Phone him while he is ironing; and do you know where the wall of the insane asylum is in Homs? All the way around the city'. He then asked me to tell some jokes. I racked my brain trying to find something that I could translate into Arabic, and that he would find funny. Finally, I came up with one.

'They were asking people around the world for their opinion on power cuts.' Nabil immediately began to laugh, the topic being rather close to his heart as power cuts, occurring practically on a daily basis, were part of life. I hushed him.

'They asked an American, 'what's your opinion on power cuts?' The American replied, 'what are power cuts?' They asked a Sudanese and he said, 'what is power?' And they asked a Syrian, 'what's your opinion on power cuts?' The Syrian replied, 'what's an opinion?'"

The joke was a success, so I tried another one, on the same theme.

'A man working on the moon (an astronaut, but I didn't know the word for that) returned to earth, and he was asked which country was the most beautiful from the moon. Without a second's hesitation he said, 'Syria, of course'. 'Syria? Why?' He was asked by everyone, astonished. 'Because,' he replied, 'Syria is just like a Christmas tree, with lights going on and off, on and off all the time.'

Nabil laughed again and called the waiter over to order some dessert. When it arrived, it turned out to be a dry, date-filled round pastry with a generous proportion of essentially uncooked meringue to pour over it. As we munched our way through this I decided to throw caution to the winds and relate a more politically-oriented joke.

'On the morning after the election (the Syrian Presidential election of December 1991) the President was sitting up in bed reading the morning papers. His secretary came in and said, 'Good Morning Monsieur le President, you must be a very happy man today, no? You have received 99.982 per cent of the vote. Ninety-nine point nine eight two! Only 741 people voted against you, Monsieur le President! What more can you want? What more can you want?' The President put down his paper and said, 'their names'."

Nabil gave me a steely look, as if daring me to laugh at the President's expense, pretending to be affronted and insulted. Then he began to laugh.

We discussed the election for a bit, as we both had stories to tell about how people voted twice and three times, how voting papers were not actually available at polling booths so the people manning the booths simply took the names of the voters, promising to fill the papers in for them later. Layla had been solicited near one voting booth and when she explained that she had already voted, the man responded that that was OK, she could come in and vote again! On television there had been advertisements showing people who may be illiterate how to fill the papers in. The tick went into the box marked 'yes'. The President, Hafez Al-Assad, was the only candidate, so the choices were 'yes' or 'no'.

The restaurant was emptying now, yet the singer had just arrived. He came over to chat to Nabil in between songs. We sat back now, conversation slowly fading, and listened to the music. Nabil ordered some coffee.

When we finally got up to leave, it was one o'clock in the morning and the restaurant was empty. The waiters and servers were lounging at two tables almost, but not quite, outside our line of vision and several of them were eating their supper. As we walked out the singer waved to us and continued singing to a now non-existent audience.

Although it was winter and the middle of the night, we opted to walk home. The sky overhead was almost white-coloured, hinting at snow that in fact never arrived. Yet the air was not too chilly, and home was only a brisk 12-minute walk.

On reaching the apartment building, Nabil asked if I would like him to wait in the street until I reached my apartment. I could stick my head out over the balcony or, in my case (as the balcony is not visible from the street) out of the stairwell window to say all was well. 'You never know,' he threatened me, 'who may be waiting for you on the stairs.' I declined telling him that I would have felt safe walking alone from Wanas to my home, even at one in the morning.

Security

Whenever I talk to foreigners living outside the Middle East, their first concern is of security. 'What was it like to live in Syria?' is generally the first question, and their interest turns to disbelief when I wax enthusiasm about the country, as it was then. 'But surely it was dangerous, living there?' they always ask. At the time, television and newspapers reported explosions and bombings, and the general perception of Syria was that she was at constant war with Israel. Then there is Lebanon just a stone's throw away and, since the Iraqi army received a beating over the Kuwait incident in 1990-91, Syria was reputed to have the strongest army in the Middle East, Israel excepted.

Should you have chosen to notice, there was a strong military presence in Syria, with army vehicles driving up and down the highways and ill-concealed military aircraft hangers in the desert (visible from official roads). The standard school uniform throughout the country was military green, which instilled a military awareness into children at an early age. However, at the time that I lived there, one felt very safe in Syria. When Nabil walked me home I felt in no danger and I had, many times, walked alone at night in Aleppo, something I would never do in most other places in the world. Syria had capital punishment for rape and murder - offenders were publicly hung (early in the morning) - and the extended family social system tended to reduce the incidence of crime. Even minor thefts were treated seriously, and shame would be cast on a whole family, so each member tried to ensure that family honour was maintained. Unfortunately, in some cases the code of family honour could be taken too far. Girls had been known to be killed as a result of illicit relationships before marriage. Such stories were not necessarily restricted to the Moslem community.

Police and secret police were visible throughout Aleppo (the secret police were distinguishable by the licence plates on their Range Rover cars, which were hand painted numbers on black boards, with curtains on the back windows and photographs of President Hafez Al-Assad on most of the other windows. In other words, they were not terribly secret) and security was well maintained. During the scuffles between the government and the Moslem brotherhood (culminating with the army moving into Hama, a pretty town on the banks of the Orontes River about two hours drive south of Aleppo, and killing an estimated 20,000 people in 1982) curfews were frequently called in Aleppo. The whole city was wrapped in darkness during those times except the Christian suburbs, including Selemanieh, where the curfew had not been imposed.

People living during the unsettled 1980s always had stories to tell about killing and rioting. However, the battles seemed to touch the Christian community little, as they mostly involved the Moslem brotherhood against the government. The Syrian Constitution was secular, although the President had to be Moslem, and as the Baath Party was dominated by members of the Alawi sect (a branch of Shi'ite Moslems), a minority group in Syria, other minority groups - including Christians - tended to be well treated. Clashes between the government and the Moslem brotherhood did not reach Selemanieh.

A Christian friend of mine did his military service during those troubled years and he told me about an incident at the artillery school in Aleppo one day in June 1979 while he was there. Members of the Moslem brotherhood stormed the barracks and slaughtered everyone (around 60 cadets) that was an Alawi. The Christians weren't touched.

The animosity between the Sunnis and the Shiites (in particular the Alawi) really stemmed from the Baath Party revolution in 1963, which essentially replaced the traditional Sunni elite of the country, who were primarily absentee landlords and urban merchants, with a 'new' elite of Alawi, a minority comprising approximately 11 per cent of the population. During the French mandate period, this new elite had been looked down on as poor, landless peasants and slaves. Of course, this also provided a fertile ground for a new Baath ideology that started as many revolutions do – through café discussions in the 1940s – promising land reform and 'war' on oppressive landlords.

The Baath Party did deliver land reform, as well as industrialisation and centralised planning. Syria was transformed and integrated, and new opportunities became available in regions that had been neglected. Life in the countryside was revolutionised and gave the ruling party a rural constituency. This provided the Syrian Government with ongoing support even when many ill-conceived and unsuccessful economic policies failed.

By the time I moved to Syria the situation was calm. Even during the Gulf War in 1990-91 things were quiet. The Syrian government actively participated in the war on the side of the Americans, although the population in general sympathised with Saddam Hussein. Yet, on the day war began, January 17, expatriate blond-haired (English and American) friends of mine shopped quietly and happily in the souk.

Another story indicates the active police presence in Syria at that time. It was during 1992, when I was living in Shahaba, a more expensive Moslem district. For some weeks our quarter had been plagued by a group of stray dogs who set about howling for hours every night. A consultant from England arrived and took residence in the apartment above mine. He was slight of build, in his early 40s and was, by his own admission, a graduate from the private school-Cambridge University institution. Despite his conservativeness, he embarked on a crash Arabic-speaking course with private lessons, although the only word he seemed to be able to grasp and retain was 'kalb', meaning dog.

The howling dogs quickly got to him and he found himself operating on a round of sleepless nights followed by a night of sleep through sheer exhaustion. I suspect endless dinner parties probably did not help the situation.

Finally, one night he could stand it no longer. Donning his private-school dressing gown and slippers over striped pyjamas, he ran out into the road and chased after the dogs, throwing stones at them. It was about 3a.m. and the world was, well if not asleep, at least in bed. Within two minutes a police car screeched around the corner and two officers leaped out to grab the Englishman who, in the meantime, had tried to dart behind a parked car to hide. He was still holding a couple of stones, his dressing gown cord hung between his legs and his blood-shot eyes were wild.

'Kalb, kalb,' he screeched at the policemen.

The moral of this story is really that 1) the police were on the scene within minutes of something unusual occurring, and 2) Syrian police were friendly and understanding enough not to shoot out of hand someone apparently completely deranged who dared to call them dogs. (It should be added that, after explanations were made - with difficulty due to none of the police speaking any English - they just laughed and released the Englishman to return to bed. The howling abated somewhat after that and finally stopped altogether. Maybe the dogs were shot.)

We were always told that if we ever had problems, to go to the police. In Syria the system of blood money (or eye for eye system) still existed. If you killed someone, you or your family would have to pay the relatives of the victim or risk having someone killed in vengeance. Of course, the government tried to prevent such occurrences by throwing offenders in prison, but not all families accepted prison as a valid punishment. If you caused an accident, your safest place was with the police. They would put you in jail, but at least you couldn't be killed. Generally, you would remain in prison until the person you injured came out of hospital, or if you killed someone, until the blood money had been paid.

A friend of mine, fortunately reasonably fluent in Arabic, pulled out to overtake a stationary bus one day and hit a teenager who ran out in front of him. The teenager's legs were broken. Although it wasn't my friend's fault, the crowd around the bus immediately descended onto him with a growl of rage. My friend yelled to the crowd, 'look, before you kill me, let's get this kid to hospital.' They bundled him into the car and my friend paid the hospital bills.

That doesn't mean that no-one ever had any problems. It seems that whenever foreign women got together, someone would bring up some story about hassles, but I think it had something to do with attitude and presence. Whenever I went downtown shopping with a particular Syrian girlfriend of mine, we inevitably ran into problems with men trying to touch us. However, she tended to hang onto my arm - many women did this when they walked together - and she looked scared. With Layla I never had any problems, but she walked out forcefully and confidently, leaving me almost running to keep up with her.

Just three times in my whole time in Syria did I encounter a 'sexual' harassment. The first was walking home late at night in Shahaba when a young man came up behind me on a motor scooter and put his hand between my legs. I turned and swore at him in Arabic, momentarily debating whether to pull him off the bike and bash him. I wasn't actually frightened. I decided not to and, instead, opened the nearest gate, slammed it in his face, glared at him and strode purposefully towards the building like this was where I lived, praying the door would open. I waited five minutes then continued home. Another time the same sort of thing occurred at Telal, a major shopping area, and the pervert was a kid. I turned around to chase him and he ran off.

The third time occurred one evening after I stopped to buy a chicken for dinner. As I was walking away three men, aged around 20, came up to me. One tried to put his arm around me. I ignored him and kept walking. Another (or the same man, I'm not sure) tried pulling my bag off my shoulder and a third pulled my hair. I turned around and screamed at them: 'bas ba'a khalas' (which essentially means 'piss off') and they stopped. I heard a man on a nearby street stall say something like, 'hey, she speaks Arabic'. This can be roughly translated to mean 'she's not really a foreigner, so leave her alone'.

However, I think the best story about safety in Syria came from a comment made by my father. In 1991 when I was planning to move to Syria, I suggested my parents drive with me from Europe. They were keen on the idea of the trip, however said there was no way in this lifetime that they would enter Syria itself. They would drive with me to Ankara in Turkey and then fly home.

The only flights available were too expensive so, after a lot more persuasion, I managed to get them to agree to enter Syria. Having managed that, I then worked on getting a few days of sightseeing out of them. After all, I had been to Syria already and knew how safe it was.

Our trip from Europe would probably provide enough subject matter for a whole other book. Anyway, they had a good time in Syria and left the country not having experienced any particularly sinister adventures.

About a year later I went to Iran for a conference. In those days it was almost impossible to make international telephone calls from Syria, so I always tried to call home when I went to Turkey or almost anywhere else outside of Syria. The day before leaving Iran, I rang my parents and my dad answered.

'Where are you calling from?' he asked after the hellos and how are you were done.

'I'll give you a hint,' I replied. 'I'm dressed from head to foot in black'.

'That's not much of a hint.'

'I'm in Teheran.'

There was a sudden, foreboding silence from the other end of the telephone.

'It's a wonderful country,' I gushed. 'The people are so friendly and...'

'If.. you.. say.. so', my father replied, very slowly and deliberately. I think he imagined that I was speaking with a gun to my head. 'When are you leaving?'

'Tomorrow night.'

'Straight to Damascus?'

'Yes.'

'Syrian airlines?'

'Yes.'

'You know, your mother and I were delighted to get your letter telling us all about your trip to Lebanon, knowing that when you wrote it you were safely back in Syria. We will be equally happy to hear from you again after your return to Aleppo.'

Perhaps, in my father's eyes, the bar was set rather low – what would have been considered the safest place between Iran, Lebanon and Syria? However, his words certainly suggested that, having visited Syria, my parents now viewed it as a safe enough place for their daughter to live.

Washing

In our apartment washing clothes was a major hassle. To begin with, we had no washing machine and laundrettes did not exist in Syria. Getting everything professionally washed or dry cleaned, although inexpensive by European standards, was impractical and beyond our means. Most of the time we had to hand wash our things.

Every family had to wash clothes and the bigger the family, the correspondingly larger the accumulated volume of dirty laundry. It seemed that in Selemanieh most families did washings nearly every day. Drying clothing and sheets could be seen dangling from nearly every balcony in the city and lines often overhung downstairs neighbours' balconies. Our downstairs neighbours actually had awnings over their balcony, which was a big relief to me the first time I washed my things. There was the inevitable dripping: after all, hand washed items have not had the advantage of a spin cycle. However, I was not prepared for the bombardment of abusive language from the woman downstairs as she craned her head around the awning and complained of the fact that the clothes were dripping onto her awning. I shrugged my shoulders and apologised. Before going indoors, I glanced up at our upstairs neighbours washing which overhung our balcony. Sure, it dripped slightly but the water was clean, even if it hit me on the head.

The following week I did my washing early in the morning, hanging it out at 6a.m. At 6.05a.m. there was some banging on the door. Opening it, I perceived our downstairs neighbour sporting blue and white striped pyjamas. His thick eyebrows and droopy, greying moustache were all tousled with sleep. He looked furious.

'I'm sleeping on the balcony and the water is dripping onto my face,' he said. I apologised and removed the clothes. It was a big mistake.

For the next couple of weeks, I was not often home and managed to get things washed properly at a friend's house. However, Layla had problems every single time she tried to hang things out or to wash the balcony. She finally got very annoyed at them and things calmed down.

One day, when I'd been in the apartment about six weeks, I started to do my washing at 10a.m. One of the major inconveniences of our apartment was the necessity of pumping all the water up to it, using an electrical pump that made some noise. Many of the apartments in our building had them, including our lovely downstairs neighbours. I turned on the pump and began washing.

I had just hung out my underwear - after carefully squeezing all the water out of them - and was rinsing some tops when there was the now familiar banging on the door (we had a doorbell, but they never used it). I thought to myself, 'no, I can't believe it. The underwear isn't even dripping.' I ignored the door. The banging continued, so I opened it. It was the woman.

She began berating me in Arabic, so I raised my voice slightly and explained that I was sorry but we had no washing machine so we had to hand wash everything and so there would be some dripping but that was normal. We had no choice. I added that there was no dripping for the moment anyway. What was she complaining about?

'No,' she said in Arabic. 'Listen. You can hear the pump. It is making too much noise. Turn it off.'

At that I got mad. No pump equals no washing equals no dripping. Besides, we were entitled to use the pump as much as we liked. I forgot my Arabic and yelled at her in English.

'That is too much. Get out.'

She looked at me, clearly understanding what I had said through the tone in my voice. 'Get out?'

'Yes, get out.' I shoved her back through the doorway and slammed the door in her face. I then deliberately kept the pump running longer than usual and let my clothes drip.

That evening a bemused male cousin of Layla's arrived at our flat.

'I was just walking up the stairs when I got accosted by a woman on the floor below. She asked me, 'do you know those girls upstairs?' I replied yes and she began telling me that one of them had been insulting her and using foul language.'

Well, foul language or not, it had the desired effect for some weeks, until Layla did a washing herself one morning. Two drips onto the awning below and the door was banged on. She ignored it totally. The banging continued, and then it seemed that someone was kicking the door.

'I thought he was going to kick the door down completely,' she told me later. So, she finally opened the door and, without waiting for a word from the man, launched into him with such a tirade of words and abuse that he returned downstairs and ever since the only acknowledgment we got from them was a look of studied disapproval when we met on the stairs. We always said 'Marhaba,' (hello) but they didn't deign to reply. However, they no longer complained about drips or pumps either.

The Accident

Syrian roads were a nightmare. The drivers had no inclination to worry about tomorrow and their most precious instrument was the horn, which they used constantly. The quickest way to gain experience in Syrian driving habits was to take a local bus inter-city. These buses were extremely well decorated; in fact, it was a wonder the drivers could see out at all, as they covered the front windows with all manner of ornaments. Often a well-endowed woman was prominent, although she was always decently covered. Otherwise, popular decorations were recitations from the Koran - presumably to counteract any possibility of accident - flowers, bobbles and the original dromedary necklaces. Thus, decorations covered most of the windows and cracks and dirt filled in the spaces. In addition, each local bus - as opposed to the more up-market types which commanded advance bookings - was equipped with at least two horns. One seemed to say 'Hi there, how are you today', while the other definitely left no room to manoeuvre. It announced, with its resounding blast, 'get out of my way or I'll smash you to pieces'. Almost any vehicle on a Syrian road, barring petrol tankers, deferred to such buses, as they plied the roads at 100 km/hour or more.

Taxis were not much better. Some drivers were very good, however most of them took Allah into their hearts and acceleration into their feet. Only once was I in an accident in a taxi, Allah karim (God is generous), and only because it seemed that, other than their horns - the most important item in a car - taxi drivers kept their brakes in perfect working order. My taxi accident occurred because the driver spent more time using his rear-view mirror to gaze at me than in watching the road. Consequently, he reduced his chances of applying his brakes in time to nil. We knew in advance we would have an accident. Fortunately, it was only a minor dent.

While I was living in Syria there were other stories where people were not so lucky. Leaving ICARDA, where I worked, one afternoon we saw a taxi, completely smashed, in the middle of the dual carriageway road. The following day, we met an Australian couple who was able to tell us exactly what had happened to the taxi.

They had started their trip on a bus in Damascus. The bus driver had played 'chicken' with a convoy of trucks heading to Turkey for much of the trip from Damascus to Hama. According to the Australian couple, the bus had almost tipped over several times. Anyway, that part of the trip came to a sudden end not far from Hama when the bus blew a tire. They walked into Hama along with others from the bus, including a Jewish couple from Damascus. They all piled into taxis: the Australian couple was going to travel with the Jewish couple, however the Jewish couple had too much luggage so they couldn't all fit into the one taxi. The Australian couple took the second taxi and were directly behind the Jewish couple's taxi when it also blew a tire and flipped. The driver and the Jewish couple were killed. They stopped to see if there was anything that could be done, and witnessed another vehicle stop and its occupants loot all the luggage from the crashed taxi.

It was always a bit disconcerting when pulling out to overtake a slow vehicle on the motorway, to find a horse and cart ambling towards you in your passing lane. Syrians preferred to take the easiest path, so why cross over onto the other side of the road? In fact, during the three years I lived in Syria, Syrian drivers began to get used to dual-carriageway roads and to adhere more to the correct side of the road. Traffic lights, too, began to be accepted objects to obey rather than being simply treated as decorations. It did remain difficult, though, to judge whether it was better to run a red light in order to avoid being hit by the car immediately behind you, or to stop in order to avoid a collision with cars coming from the other road.

However, I did once have a real accident. This occurred during my first months in Syria when I still had my own car, which was a 1976 Range Rover. Presidential Election fever was high and demonstrations (in favour of the President, of course) rife. I had been to Arabic classes and was giving the teacher, Suheila, a lift home. At the same time as the demonstrations - masses of cars waving patriotic flags - there was a convoy of trucks transiting through Syria from Turkey to Jordan. These trucks, as they all had to move at the same time with a police/customs escort, blocked most of the main road and the demonstrating vehicles managed the rest. We got stuck in a horrendous traffic jam, inching forward a metre at a time.

Syrians were normally quite patient: they could sit for hours doing nothing other than contemplate life. However, once behind the wheel of a vehicle, they would become like demons. In cars, they had no patience at all and a delay of one or two seconds would drive them crazy. They would honk and shout and rev their engines and move into any available space, trying to reach a gap in the traffic first. Of course, this practice usually made any traffic jam worse and one often wondered how such jams could be untangled without the help of a helicopter to pull the vehicles out. All manner of vehicles would seem to be locked together like a jigsaw puzzle.

I guess, therefore, that the accident was really my fault. I did not try to move right up behind the car in front, as I had turned my engine off. We had not moved for some minutes and the cars inching in front had created a space of some five metres. Suddenly, the Peugeot in front of me lost patience and evidently decided to try extricating itself by the back route. The engine revved and the car reversed towards us at a rapidly accelerating rate.

I just had time to say to Suheila, 'hey, he's going to hit us,' before he actually did so. Fortunately, the Range Rover is a good, solid vehicle. I climbed out to survey the damage. There was a touch of white paint on my thick black bumper but nothing else and I saw with a quick glance of satisfaction that the other car's rear taillight was smashed and the back slightly dented. It would teach him a lesson. I fixed my face into a severe glare, gave it to him, turned my back and made to go. However, he caught my arm and began shouting at me.

He was a large man with a protruding belly, the inevitable moustache and a thick head of black hair balding at the crown. He was dressed in army green, covered by a civilian coat.

Suheila came to the rescue. She told the man it was his fault and therefore we had nothing to do with it. He yelled back that I would have to pay for the damage to his car. After a few minutes of such an exchange of words, I turned on the engine of my car and told Suheila we were getting out of there, as gaps had been created in the traffic. The man returned to his car.

However, he did not let us leave. All he did was reverse his car again so that my own had no way of moving and it was then that I caught a glimpse of the colour of his license plate; it had green letters. In other words, the man was an important employee of the government. Suheila confirmed this by informing me that he was in fact a general in the Syrian Army.

At that time, there were different coloured licence plates in Syria for different classes of cars. Black letters on white plates were normal, privately-owned cars; red on white signified commercial vehicles, such as taxis. Green on white were government vehicles and blue on white/white on blue were for cars owned by foreigners or foreign companies. The addition of a red line signified an international organisation. Finally, white lettering on black was reserved for the secret police.

In the meantime, a police officer had wandered over to us. The army general began yelling at him as well and Suheila added to the din by trying to explain what had really happened. The general was evidently piling all the blame onto me. I was a woman and a foreigner, two reasons why I should not be driving at all. The policeman asked for my car papers, so I showed him my passport and the car's 'carnet de passage' (the car still had European licence plates). The general tried to take the carnet de passage, so I grabbed it back. We began a tug of war with it, but I was not going to let him have it. After some 10 seconds, I gave an extra tug and won. Then the policeman informed me I should accompany him to the station.

Suheila protested: it was not my fault, but the general was throwing his weight about - not difficult, he was certainly amply provided - and the policeman said it was the best way to regulate things quickly. He climbed into the back of the Range Rover and directed us to the station.

The station was a large, multi-storeyed block with long, badly lit corridors. Perhaps during the day it would contain more life, however at that moment, about 7p.m., the corridors were empty and office doors shut. We climbed three flights of stairs and were ushered into an office, where a uniformed man sat at the other end behind a largely empty desk. A photograph of the President, Hafez Al-Assad, stared down at me from the back wall with a sterner look than usual.

Suheila launched into an animated explanation of the accident and the man seemed well-disposed to listen. He even smiled slightly and said that everything could probably be sorted out happily. We were escorted out again and taken up another flight of stairs to another office.

This office contained three desks, all filled with bored-looking young men, and about six arranged in a line in the centre of the room. We sat down on these. One of the young men asked for my papers and I handed them to him while Suheila gave her explanation again. Then the general arrived. He launched into another of his tirades and at the end of it insisted that I pay for the damage to his car. He wanted 5000 Syrian pounds ($100 US).

Suheila said it was ridiculous, it wasn't even my fault. More arguments ensued. The general picked up my papers, rifled through them and asked for my driver's licence.

This was the one item I did not have on me, as it had been sent to Beirut so my international licence could be renewed. This was explained.

'So, she's driving without a licence,' the general roared. 'Throw her in prison.'

I had not understood, of course, but Suheila's face turned white and when she translated it to me I felt scared for the first time. Until that moment, I had not really considered myself in any danger. I had always felt quite safe in Syria and my experiences with policemen anywhere had mostly been good. Besides, the gentleman downstairs had been kind. I tried, through Suheila, to tell them they were being silly.

'Throw her in prison,' the general insisted. 'She should stay in prison until she can produce a driver's licence.' The young men around seemed powerless to do anything. The general was an important person, it seemed, and they were obliged to follow his orders. Somewhat shakily, I asked if I could use the telephone.

Suheila and I began trying to track down various people at ICARDA, in particular the man who took care of all transport problems, including customs clearance etc. He was well-known to the police and had very good relations with them. His name was Mustapha and he was, in my mind, one of the most efficient and able employees at ICARDA. The hugest man I had ever seen, he was the proud father of four young children and despite being in an extremely stressful job could always find a smile and a pleasant word. As a side-line he sold track suits and I once saw him, during a very brief period when he thought of trying to lose some weight, running in bright orange one. He really looked like an orange rolling along the road.

We were unable to track him down directly, as he was relaxing by a pool table somewhere. However, his wife promised to send him over as soon as she located him. In the meantime, I got hold of a neighbour of ours - I was staying with a girlfriend at the time - and tried to explain where my national driver's licence was located in the apartment, so my girlfriend could dig it out when she got home. It might help, although they really wanted the international one. I wondered how long it would take to return from Beirut. In other words, I wondered how many evenings I would end up sleeping here, at the police station - or in prison.

The general kept up his unpleasantness. He really was determined to make me suffer. Suheila began discussing with the young men exactly how much damage had been done to the car and it transpired that the damage was minimal and would only cost some 1500 Syrian pounds - about $30 US - to repair. While Suheila was translating this part of the conversation to me, the general left the room.

The atmosphere immediately lightened. The young men smiled, and one offered us some tea. I talked to Suheila, who then turned to the young men, and said;

'You know, if it is only going to cost 1500 pounds to fix the car, I'm sure I can persuade this girl to pay that. The 5000 being demanded earlier was far too much, but I'm sure she would be willing to pay 1500. Why don't I ask her to pay that and then you can let us go. It is all the man wants, surely.'

Of course, I was willing to pay 1500 pounds. By that stage I was willing to pay 5000, even though my sense of fair play exploded against it as I had not been at fault. However, I was now scared and also very tired. I had been in the rural areas of Syria all day and I wanted to get home, have a shower and go to bed. I also wanted to eat, as it was now 9p.m. and we had been in the police station nearly two hours.

The young men replied that the money was not the only problem. Of course, I had to pay, my not having a licence meant that the accident was definitely my fault. But the general also wanted me to go to prison for the night, as a sort of lesson, and they were powerless to refuse. I would have to spend the night in prison.

Suheila translated this and I digested it. I'd never seen the inside of any prison, so I asked Suheila what it might be like. Would there be a section for women? What would happen? I could not imagine that it would be so horrific as all that. I had heard stories of prisons throughout the Middle East, but could it really be that bad? I guessed it possibly could and I fought back tears of fright.

Finally, Suheila stood up and moved towards the desks where the three men sat.

'Look,' she said, in a pleading yet persuasive voice. 'Look at what you are doing. Look at this young girl, she is a visitor to our country, a student. She is working here, in our country, day and night. She works day and night, seven days a week to help develop the agriculture of our country. She has come here, on her own, all the way from New Zealand, to help us, to help us develop our country and you want to put her in prison.

'You all know the accident was not her fault. She is just a young girl. Think. Think of your families. Would you want to see your sisters or your daughters being put into prison for the night? Would you want to see this happen? She is just a visitor to our country. How can you treat her in this way?'

If violins had sounded at that moment the scene would have been perfect. I could almost detect a fumbling for the handkerchiefs as the young men sat, almost in tears. After a long, long silence, one of them coughed.

'OK,' he said. 'You can go home.'

'Thank you, sir,' Suheila replied. She turned to me. 'We can go.'

I asked no questions. I did not know what she had said, I only found out later. I just got up, said 'Shukran' (thank you) to the men, gave them a wan smile and collected my passport and papers. As we left the young man told us to ensure that Mustapha passed by, either that night or the next day, in order to regulate payment.

We trooped down the four flights of stairs, hardly able to believe it. I kept a grim, frightened look on my face in case we met anyone (particularly the general), but once outside I laughed and laughed.

We bundled ourselves into the car and, while driving to Suheila's house, she told me, verbatim, what she had said. I was still a little shaky, but I felt in a sort of euphoria, a sort of high. It was possibly hunger and fatigue and perhaps the adrenalin that had come with fear. I could not stop laughing, almost hysterically.

I ate at Suheila's house and telephoned around to announce my safety. Of course, in hindsight I probably would not have gone to prison, as I am sure the ICARDA umbrella would have saved me. In fact, Mustapha turned up at the station shortly after we had left and regulated everything. It did cost me something, but in fact in the end even less than the demanded 1500 pounds, as Mustapha organised that I purchase a replacement for the broken taillight and the general paid for the rest of the damage. However, I do wonder how I would have managed if Suheila had not been there.

By the time I left Suheila's house, utter and total fatigue had taken me over completely. Shock had also hit me and so did the realisation that without Suheila I would still be at the police station. Moreover, it was Suheila who had had the telephone numbers. Had I been on my own I could have contacted no-one, and I would probably have been put into prison. At that moment I hated Syria and Syrians: the general was prominent in my mind. Then I got lost, and drove for about 10 minutes in mindless circles, trying to locate some familiar landmark. I hated Syria even more.

Finally, I stopped and flagged down a taxi to ask him for directions. He indicated that I should follow him and as we approached the Pullman Hotel, he tooted and did an about turn, driving quickly away in his previously intended direction, without ever once asking for payment of any sort. Suddenly I loved Syria again and especially its people. They were so friendly and helpful. They were wonderful.

Balcony sitting

Late one Saturday afternoon I was bored with nothing to do. I hadn't been out of the apartment all day, and now there was a power cut, forcing me to stop work on my portable computer. I changed from my sloppy indoor clothes and took the seven-minute walk to Basel's house.

As I turned onto Basel's street, I saw his mother lean out over the balcony and wave to me. I found both the outside and the apartment doors open and as I pushed into the apartment Basel's mother, Oom Akram (mother of Akram. Syrian parents are often called after their eldest son), called me out onto the balcony. I closed the apartment door and joined her.

Basel was not there just at that moment, she announced, but not to worry, I was to sit down, enjoy the sights and she would get me some tea.

From my newly acquired vantage point on the balcony, I felt in touch with the world. I could look across and into the apartment opposite, where its occupants seemed to move constantly from one room to another. I could just make out a television in the corner. Basel's district had a different power cut schedule to ours.

On the street below I watched the butcher mince what would be his final sale for the day. Basel had already pointed out that butcher to me as someone to avoid, as he snuck in lower-grade imported lamb and passed it off as Awassi, the local fat-tailed sheep breed considered the best quality by Syrians. Basel had told me that from the balcony they used to watch him bring the meat in, and I now realised he was right. The balcony was a perfect place from which to observe such goings on.

Oom Akram returned with the tea and a plate of pistachios. She sat down and immediately began pointing out people and sights to me.

'There's the man who owns the shop just around the corner. He's married to the sister of our neighbour two floors up.... You see those people? They had a huge fight in the street the day before yesterday, something about non-payment of a service. It seems they are talking again. Oh look, that is the third time this week that that woman has visited that apartment. I've seen her sitting on the balcony over there. Oom George from upstairs said she is checking out the daughter that lives there as a possible husband for her son... Oh, I haven't seen Oom Nabil in ages, and there she is! Marhaba! Marhaba!' She leaned precariously over the balcony, calling to a passing woman, stoutly dressed in a fancy two-piece knit, who stopped and yelled back. Oom Akram began frantically inviting her up but, after five minutes of protestations, Oom Nabil managed to escape, by virtue of a floor between her and her adversary.

A donkey cart ambled up the street with long steel rods piled behind. The driver pulled the donkey to a halt and began off-loading the rods. Several cars pulled into the street and a taxi stopped to let a passenger out.

'He just got married last week. He and his new wife live over there.' Oom Akram pointed the apartment out to me.

I suddenly felt like an actress in an Alfred Hitchcock movie, observing the movements of all the neighbours around the district. Clutching my arm suddenly, Oom Akram pointed to another woman that had just turned into the road. There were rumours about her. Apparently, she was not a 'nice' girl at all.

That remark reminded me of the rumours that had flown around our apartment building about a month after our arrival. Our upstairs neighbours had invited themselves to coffee one morning when I was not there and had asked Layla who the fat man in the white car was that always drove me home. As I had been dropped off at the apartment on some half dozen occasions during that month, and as most of the ICARDA cars were white, they were obviously talking about me. However, it had not been one but several different people, and the only one even remotely 'fat' was about to retire, being older than my father. Furthermore, his daughter had usually been with us when dropping me off.

When Layla asked our neighbours to be a little more specific in the description of the man so she could put a name to him, the neighbours had replied,

'Oh, we never actually saw the man or the car. We just heard about it.'

Oom Akram continued a monologue on the history and gossip concerning almost everyone that passed in the street below. Only once did she murmur, 'I don't know them at all. Who can they be?'

The buzzer sounded from the entrance below but, rather than move back to speak through the intercom, she simply craned her neck over the balcony to cry to the potential visitor below. It was a friend of Basel's, who decided not to come up as Basel was not at home.

During a lull in movement in the street, Oom Akram turned the subject towards her neighbour's ways of hanging out washing. There were several examples visible, and she pulled these to pieces. Hanging out washing is an art, she informed me. Sheets and towels and other large items should always go to the front, and should be perfectly straight, military fashion. Smalls should always be hidden behind. Everything should be colour coordinated.

There was a knock at the door and Basel's mother rushed to answer. I sat back and gazed down the street to the dying rays of sunlight hitting one of the apartment blocks at the end of the road. The rays were turning the stone buildings a hazy red colour as the sun, out of my sight, disappeared from the horizon. Slowly slowly, lights began to appear at the windows of many of the apartments. Behind me, Oom Akram flicked the light switch, immediately darkening the sky outside. With her was Oom George, the upstairs neighbour. As usual, Oom George was wearing a dressing gown and slippers, despite the fact that she had left her own home. Oom Akram, too, was wearing only a nightie. She gathered up our teacups and went off to make some coffee. Oom George joined me on the balcony and took up the running commentary of happenings in the street at roughly the place where Oom Akram had left off. I had already met Oom George and it was a delight to chat to her as she spoke fluent, if rusty, French, having once been a pupil at a Catholic School run by Nuns.

The coffee arrived and the two neighbours began pooling their resources of recent gossip concerning all their neighbours. It suddenly occurred to me that, at that very moment, other groups of people we could see on other balconies could well be gossiping about us and in particular about this foreigner, this ajinabieh, that came calling all the time on Basel and his family.

As we finished our coffee, we turned our cups upside down in the saucers to allow all of the gunk at the bottom of the cup to drain away. As they did so, they left drying patterns of coffee sludge around the sides of the cups. One by one, Oom George lifted them up and read our fortunes. Patterns in my cup signified a bird, which meant good news or a letter, and a long unbroken line, meaning that I would travel soon. The cup could not lie. I was overdue for a letter from my mother and I had a trip to the desert organised for the following week.

As I mused over my forthcoming good luck, Basel walked in and laughed at me peering into my cup. However, he said seriously, 'Oom George is an expert on cup reading.' She and Oom Akram certainly spent a long time over their own cups, planning their movements over the next few days based on what they read in the coffee dregs.

Basel had been shopping for food, so on his return his mother grabbed the plastic bags and disappeared into the kitchen to sort everything out. Rarely would she go shopping. In fact, few women would shop for basic necessities if there was a man in the house. Oom Akram tended to give Basel a list of things to purchase and he did all the shopping, including such items as shampoo and hair dyes that his mother needed.

As it was now dark, we also moved indoors and, while Oom Akram filled the fridge with food, Basel grabbed a chopping board and a knife and began cutting up the 30 rounds of bread that he had purchased. Each round was pulled apart, cut in half and made up into convenient sized piles of some 20 pieces, which would be frozen. This would keep the bread fresh, and rounds could be removed from the freezer and held over the gas hobs for a minute or so to thaw and soften them, as required.

Oom Akram came in to grab the bread as Basel completed cutting it up and informed me that I was staying to dinner. I protested, saying that Layla was planning dinner and I was expected home. Oom Akram mumbled in derision and annoyance and I could read her mind, which asked how dared I not stay to dinner? Besides, Layla would have no real idea how to cook - I would be better fed where I was. Therefore, she argued the point for a bit, but eventually conceded as I stood up to walk out of the apartment.

Oom Akram was not really wrong in her musings; it was normal for visitors to stay to dinner - and for the night, and for breakfast, lunch, for several days, for a week - no questions would have been asked. And her doubts on Layla's proficiency as a cook were also justified. She knew Layla would not be able to cook because Layla was not married, and unmarried women did not know how to cook. In fact, most Christian girls were spared household duties prior to their marriage and were practically waited on, hand and foot, by their mothers. The tradition in the Christian community was for the girl's mother to teach her daughter how to cook and manage a household after the wedding. If the couple had moved to a different town, the mother tended to join them for a short period while the bride learned these skills.

I always laughed at Layla when her parents visited, because her mother inevitably took over the kitchen. She would wash and iron Layla's clothes - and my own if I let her - and would always leave a fridge full of food, generally home-cooked. However, Layla was able to cook one dish - well, two really - and this was what she planned to prepare for that evening.

When I arrived at the apartment, I found Layla and two friends sitting on our balcony drinking coffee. Two pots were quietly simmering on the stove, one with a mixture of rice and spaghetti and the other with a kind of chilli con carne (without the chilli). I joined the group on the balcony and the addition of the new voice in the group quickly attracted our upstairs neighbours, who leaned over the edge of their balcony to examine the new arrival. They called 'hello' to me and then yelled over their shoulder to an unseen person in the background, 'it's just Lynne'. I was poignantly reminded of the evening that our neighbours came downstairs and demanded admittance to our apartment so as to have a better sight of the visitors we had at the time. Due to a power cut, our only form of lighting had been candles that flickered considerably in the breeze and they had not provided adequate vision for our neighbours as they leaned over the balcony.

We all opted to sit indoors to eat, so as not to have our meal discussed in the apartment above as well, although they could probably smell it quite easily.

The three Marys

I never became Syrian in my treatment of visitors. Syrians loved visiting each other and they could spend every day in the same person's house, hour after hour after hour. If several days passed without my visiting Basel's mother, she would launch a tirade of interrogatory questions as to my whereabouts the previous days and why had I not passed by much earlier. One visit to a family generated friends for life and they expected you at their doorstep each day. On the bus from work in the afternoons it was almost impossible to extricate myself from invitations to coffee and one girl in particular would count the number of times I rejected her offers, which made me feel guilty. But I knew that once inside her house, no excuse could get me out again: A quick half-hour visit for either tea or coffee was impossible. Even claims of fatigue would be met with offers of a bed.

Another friend lived with her mother and three sisters. There were no sons and the father had died. The house was always full of visitors and the girls were forever preparing cups of coffee or tea or offering fruit, chocolates or peeled cucumbers. One day they counted over 200 visitors, fortunately not all at once, but they never seemed to have time for anything other than entertaining visitors. Being European, I valued my privacy and after a day of work the last thing I wanted to do was spend hours entertaining people, unless it was a planned event.

Certainly, there were advantages to living on the fifth floor with no lift and no telephone. We didn't even have a buzzer system downstairs, which meant that any potential visitor had to actually climb the 102 stairs just to see if we were home and this obstacle deterred quite a high percentage of visitors, I think. Both Layla and I had very busy schedules and were hardly ever home, so many people, after a few wasted and useless trips, stopped coming unless by appointment.

Secondly, there were advantages to being European. Layla, having the larger number of acquaintances living nearby, had a lot of casual visitors, while my own friends tended to make appointments. Had I been Syrian, I would have been socially obliged to invite Layla's friends in, offer them coffee and make small chit chat for the socially acceptable period of time, usually a minimum of 15 minutes. I avoided this by simply informing the callers that Layla was 'ma mojoud' - not home - and looking slightly questioningly in case they had some message to impart. In any case, I held the door half closed instead of invitingly open and generally the callers got the hint and left again. As time went on some of her friends became, by extension, mine as well and if they appeared I invited them in.

There was a group of girls living in the vicinity of our apartment who tended to visit each other's houses every evening and to attend church together on Sundays. They were all in their late 20s and had never, as far as I could make out, ever had any male friends (although one once told me she had almost become engaged at one time. Of course, this did not necessarily mean that she had ever actually been out with the man). A couple of months after we moved to Selemanieh, they asked if they could visit. I accepted with alacrity and the following afternoon I purchased copious quantities of soft drinks, together with cakes and biscuits from the friendly bakery downstairs.

At 6p.m. the four girls arrived, clapping their hands in amazement at my bed-sitting room which was set out Bedouin-style with a mattress and cushions on the floor. In addition, I had woven donkey carrier bags in one corner and a low copper platter serving as a coffee table. In fact, as I informed my visitors, I slept on the mattress on the floor, as the bed was too uncomfortable. My visitors opted to sit Bedouin-style - on the rugs - rather than using the more normal sofa and chairs in the living room.

Three of the girls were wearing dresses for the occasion, while the fourth, trying to adopt a more European style of dress, had chosen jeans and a T-shirt. Bedouin style, they took their shoes off and lounged against the cushions, while the jeans-wearer, whose name was not Mary, sat cross-legged on the floor. I underline the fact that her name was not Mary, because my other three visitors had all been christened Mary, which was the most popular girl's name in the Christian part of Aleppo. Its popularity as a girl's name was possibly only surpassed by the use of Mohammed for boys amongst Moslem families.

I served tea flavoured with cinnamon, which we drank without milk, soft drinks and cakes, with everyone avidly forgetting diets for the day. Being not yet married, they were all conscious of their figures, despite the fact that the Syrian man's ideal was somewhat more rounded than the European clothes-hanger figure.

As was usual on such occasions, the talk quickly turned to the opposite sex. I realised that none of the girls would ever have had any experience with men and I therefore chose to take rather a back seat in the discussion. To begin with, they discussed a dirty joke that had circulated amongst the women on our bus earlier in the week. Such jokes were never ever told in mixed company, although as it was a new joke (along the banana line) for me, I guessed that it had probably done the rounds of the men as well. Layla had been told the joke by the only married woman on the bus, who was considered to be the group's authority on sex by virtue of her married status, despite the fact that her husband had reputedly left her after only a week, and she was once again living with her mother and sister. She had managed to give birth to a daughter, so it is assumed that she did receive the required education.

Anyway, after imparting the joke in Layla's ear, she had added the following words of wisdom: 'Men like that, you know.'

So, I found myself listening to a rather strange conversation, of three Marys and a non-Mary, sharing half understood parables of wisdom from local authorities on sex. Fortunately for my peace of mind, it did not occur to them to ask me for any explanations or comments.

'Well,' said a Mary eventually, 'there are two things that are forbidden to me in my life at present, drugs and sex. But I'm doing my best to change that.' She stopped for a second. 'For the second one only, of course,' she added.

It took me a minute to understand what she meant, but of course she meant that she was aiming to get married. Then sex would be OK.

'Yes,' said the non-Mary, 'I think your virginity is the best gift you can give your husband.'

I thought of the many stories that I had heard, for example of a woman now happily married with four children, who had managed to sleep with her husband-to-be, who was not her first lover, a couple of days before the wedding towards the end of her period. He was delighted to see the blood, didn't suspect the real reason, and, so the story goes, has remained in blissful ignorance ever since. I had also been told of girls going to specific gynaecologists to have their hymens reinstated.

'Did you hear about the girl over on—street the other day?' Mary piped up. No-one replied, so she continued, horror starting to appear in the corners of her eyes. 'They found a girl hanging. I mean, she had hung herself. Committed suicide, you know? No-one knew why because she hadn't said anything to anyone and hadn't left a note. The first thing the doctor checked, was to see if she was a virgin.'

'Well, was she?' I asked.

'I don't know,' she admitted. 'But it would have been the reason why she killed herself if she wasn't.'

'Well, I'll tell you another story.' This statement came from a different Mary, after the shocked exclamations and reactions to the other one had subsided.

'A friend of mine from Damascus - you know her, Mary,' she said, turning to the person sitting on her left, 'Huda, you know? She came up to stay some six months ago. Anyway, she has been going out with a medical student in Damascus. Well, not really going out, but they have been seeing each other for about three years. She hasn't told her parents, I don't know why. Anyway, they have, you know, slept together, and he told her that he wanted to marry her when he graduates. Well, apparently he used to go out with another girl before he met Huda. Huda knows the girl and knows that he stopped seeing her. Well, recently the other girl - I don't know if she has just found out they are going out or what, but she went to him and told him that as she was no longer a virgin and as it was him that had taken it, he had to marry her.'

'Well, so he should,' exclaimed the non-Mary.

'But what about your friend, Huda?' I asked. 'Didn't he take hers, too?'

'Yes, he did. Well, he told his ex-girlfriend that he didn't want to marry her. So, she went and told her parents that they had, you know, slept together, and her parents told his parents that unless he married their daughter, they would get the police and have him put into prison.'

I was startled. 'Is that possible?'

'Yes, it is against the law to sleep together before you get married.'

'So, what happened? Did they get married?'

'Not yet. The two families had a big meeting one night and the girl's parents - they are really mad - wanted to march them to the church there and then. Apparently they went, but he pulled out and said it wasn't possible. But his parents were now saying that he has to marry her as well. Of course, they don't know about Huda, either.'

I was getting lost. 'Wait a minute, you mean to say that we are talking about Christian families? I can't believe that anyone in such circumstances can be made to marry someone else. The girl isn't pregnant, is she?'

'No, of course not. He hasn't seen her for years. I think that she just realised that she would not be able to marry anyone else because she wasn't a virgin, and she wanted to marry him. He's a good catch, he's going to be a doctor.'

'So, what is happening?'

'Well, he told her and her parents that OK, he would marry her. But that he would never live with her, he would never have anything to do with her. Therefore, she would never have children or anything. And he is now trying to figure out a way of emigrating, and Huda plans to go with him.'

'But that is totally crazy,' I exclaimed. 'If they get married, they can't get divorced, can they?'

'Nope, they're Christian.'

'No, I can't believe it. They - I mean Huda and her friend - should go and see a Lawyer. I can't believe he can be put into prison.'

'They have seen a Lawyer, and he can be.'

'Why don't they - I mean Huda and he - elope? If he's married to someone else, then the other girl's family won't be able to do anything.'

'They could ruin his career. Huda doesn't want that to happen, either.'

Shortly after that my friends got up to leave. It was dark outside, and they didn't want to walk alone too late. They didn't have the confidence Layla and I had in the security of Aleppo's streets.

When Layla came home, I related to her the story and asked if it was possible that someone could go to prison for having taken the virginity of a woman. She assured me that it was possible. Still disbelieving I asked someone connected with law, and the response was yes, if the girl could prove who had taken her virginity. Then I thought about the penalty in Syria for rape, which is public hanging. I guess being forced to marry someone you don't want to is better than the alternative, if she should accuse you of that.

Of course, a worse outcome could be the murder of the girl. Honour killings were not unknown in Syria and this was a cultural issue, not a religious one. Even if a girl was raped, her family could take the decision to end her life in order to 'restore' the family's honour. While Mary was sure that the girl found hanging had committed suicide, it could in fact have been an honour killing.

This made the story about Huda's medical student friend and his 'ex' somewhat more unusual, as not many girls – Christian or Moslem – would admit to having had sex out of wedlock given the potential for the family to take the honour killing route. The girl must have been very sure that her parents would support her.

I was obviously curious about how this story would play out. I asked Mary from time to time what was happening in the saga. Things remained in limbo for quite some time, but one day Huda got sick of the whole thing and told her friend it was all over. As far as Mary knew, the other two had not got married, but she didn't like to ask Huda anymore.

The kiss

Shortly before I moved to Selemanieh, the Syrian government began clamping down on smuggling operations into the country. A lot of foreign goods were finding their way into shops, some by the legal method, but a lot gracing supermarket shelves had come from Lebanon, usually purchased with foreign currency that was also traded on the black market.

The most popular smuggled items - popular quantitatively speaking as they affected a larger proportion of the population - were foreign cigarettes. Syria was a nation of smokers and it had an active industry of its own. However, Syrian tobacco was rather strong and people who could afford it preferred to smoke American or British brands which could be obtained locally for about 50 pounds, or one US dollar per pack.

Sometimes foreign cigarettes were hard to get hold of and cigarette sellers had any number of ruses in order to supply their customers. Huge pockets sewn into the insides of their jackets would reveal whole boxes of the prohibited goods. These would be surreptitiously pulled out inside the shop of a valued customer and the exchange made.

Another amusing ruse was that used along one of the roads leading out of Aleppo which I often used with a work colleague who had adapted the refined habit of smoking foreign cigarettes, even though this practice cost him nearly half of his salary (he only earned the equivalent of a couple of dollars a day). Cigarette sellers - again mostly boys - would wave their packets at passing cars. We would stop and my colleague would request his preferred brand.

'One minute,' would be the reply and the seller would scoot across the road, ensure there was no traffic, loosen a rock at the side of the road and extricate a box hidden in a deep hole. Hundreds of vehicles used this road every day, their drivers little knowing that they were travelling over dozens of cachets filled with cigarettes. Climatically this practice was safe as it never rained during much of the year.

My arrival in Selemanieh coincided with a major stamp down by the government. It did not worry me as I was not a smoker, but I found myself getting asked from time to time if I could purchase some cigarettes for friends. As a foreigner, I had access to the free shop (a duty-free establishment) and the Shahaba Sham Hotel, both of which sold foreign cigarettes legally in exchange for dollars. Very few people could enter the free shop, as it was exclusively for foreigners and certain privileged sections of Syrian society, and you had to show your passport or other relevant document.

One evening I was passing the free shop and decided to buy a box of cigarettes for Basel as a surprise. I was lucky as his favourite brand was in stock: most of the time you just took what you could get, as they normally had only one or two brands available. There was a crowd of men at the counter but as usual they pulled back slightly at my arrival - my being a woman and obviously a foreigner - and allowed me to be served ahead of them. The box was going to cost 10 dollars and I had only a 20-dollar bill on me. The man behind the counter pulled a huge wad of American dollars out of his pocket - he must have had two thousand or more dollars there - and found the crispest 10 dollar note he could return to me. (Cash registers did not appear to exist.) He then handed me the box of cigarettes. I asked at another desk for a bag - I did not want to walk around holding the exposed box - and they gave me one. After completing my purchases at a couple of other shops, I headed up to Basel's house.

He was not at home. His mother was, of course, and she invited me in for a cup of tea which we sat drinking while waiting for his return. When he did, I stood up and said,

'Hi, I have a present for you.' and handed him the bag.

'Oh, thank you,' he exclaimed and leaned towards me, kissing me right on the mouth. I turned around and sat down again, unable to look at him or, more especially, his mother. Fortunately, some other people arrived just then and the moment passed.

It was some weeks before I broached the subject with him.

'Basel,' said I, one evening as we were walking along the Selemanieh road, 'Do you remember that kiss you gave me at your place? Did your mother ever say anything to you at all about it?'

'Yes she did, in fact.' I blanched.

'What did she say?'

'She asked me if that sort of thing was a regular occurrence.'

'My gosh. What did you say to her?'

'I said, 'yes, in fact'.'

Apparently, she had not been terribly approving of the fact that her son, a single man in his mid-30s, should even think of kissing a girl (also single, and also in her 30s) with whom he was not married.

On another evening Basel walked me home from dinner at his place accompanied by a niece of his who was not yet three years old and who was visiting with her parents. Her short legs pitter-pattered in the empty streets - it was late at night - and she called out loud to her 'ammo' (uncle) at regular intervals. When we reached the entrance to the apartment, the place where I would normally receive my goodnight kiss if no-one was around, Basel told his niece to give me a kiss.

'Busia Lynne. Busia Lynne, for your uncle who can't'. He did not dare to give me a kiss in front of his niece. In compensation I got a wet smack half on the cheek and half on the mouth from a little girl.

The wedding

When I first arrived in Syria, I lived for one month in a traditional courtyard house in the centre of the old city. The house was occupied by a German student, who kindly offered me temporary accommodation while I looked for something of my own. The old city was a huge cluster of tiny alleyways and twisting roads that sprawled out from the citadel in the centre of the city.

The citadel could be seen from almost everywhere in the city, as it was built on a hill with a commanding view over a large area of land. It was one of the largest citadels ever built and was always the centre, focus and defence of Aleppo. It dates back more than 2000 years, with excavations having revealed various successive conquering cultures using it, such as the Hittites (probably from as far back as the 9th century BC), Assyrians, Romans and Ayyubids.

Towards the end of the 12th century, it was converted into a medieval fortress and withstood Crusader attacks. Several famous (or infamous) Crusaders spent time as unwilling guests of the fortress, including Baldwin II, King of Jerusalem, and Reynald de Chatillon. The latter was unceremoniously put to death by Saladin, unfortunately only after he had committed many unspeakable atrocities on the local populations of modern-day Syria and Jordan.

The citadel was destroyed by the Mongols in 1260, who rebuilt it as a royal residence in 1292. By 1428, the Mamelukes controlled it, followed by the Ottoman Empire.

At the front of the citadel stood a beautifully restored three-story entrance with a throne room over the archway. The citadel was accessible over a stone causeway that was not terribly inviting to walk over if you were afraid of heights.

Aleppo's famous souks, dating from the 13th century, meandered for some 10 kilometres of covered alleyways on the other side of the road from one side of the citadel and the courtyard house where I lived was tucked down a narrow road on the opposite side of the citadel to that of the souks.

To enter the house, you had to pass through a dark alley which hid other houses behind. A heavy, padlocked, lead-based painted green door blocked the path at the far end. On entering this, a large courtyard opened out before you, with much of its yard space sheltered from the burning sun by a grape vine, its roots firmly planted in a well-watered two-metre square garden in the centre of the yard. In one corner stood an old well, a wooden bucket still resting at the edge, ready for use. Along all four walls of the courtyard were doors that opened into a conglomeration of rooms beyond. One opened into a spacious kitchen and another into a bathroom set out in European fashion: Europeans had been renting the house for years.

The building, like all those in the neighbourhood, was made from large stone blocks, grey and blackened with age. The courtyard was also paved with stone, while the floors of the rooms were mostly fabricated from fading marble tiles in intricate patterns of cream, brown and black.

By standing in one part of the courtyard and craning your neck, you could glimpse the citadel not much more than a stone's throw away. And if you were an ostrich, you could probably have seen the five mosques that surrounded the house, their loudspeakers carefully trained on the courtyard below. One only had to sleep one night in the house to realise this, as promptly at 3a.m. all five loudspeakers burst into action. Of course, they did so on four other occasions during the day as well, but somehow that never seemed to matter so much as the early morning call.

By shutting the door to the courtyard, one could shut out the world. None of the rooms had exterior windows or doors; all pointed into the courtyard. This was a traditional house, where visitors could be carefully screened, where defence was paramount and where women could be kept separate from the men if need be. Some of the rooms had interconnecting doors; there were some inner rooms only accessible through another room, and one room could only be reached by an outer stairwell. There were also huge storerooms in a basement running underneath the house, but we didn't go down there for fear of scorpions, of which there were many.

These types of courtyard houses were considered to be the nucleus of Islamic cities that had built up over 14 centuries of Arab-Islamic cultural influence. The close-knit network of back-to-back courtyard houses served by narrow alleys formed residential clusters that, together with some commercial and community buildings (such as bakeries, madrassahs – schools, mosques and hammams – bath houses) made up neighbourhoods. The social fabric of these neighbourhoods strengthened community and societal values. It used to be said that you could drop a bag in the middle of the street and several hours later it would still be there, untouched, waiting for you. During the month I lived in the courtyard house, some children climbed in over the roof one day and stole a couple of knives from the kitchen. It was interesting that that was all they took – they could have gone through all of our belongings as nothing was locked. Anyway, it became quickly known in the neighbourhood that these knives had been taken, so they were found and returned to us.

Our neighbours were all quite conservative. In the streets I never saw even the face of a woman past puberty, as all the women wore black abayas covering their whole bodies, faces included. Consequently, I dressed quite conservatively also, wearing long-sleeved tops and either loose trousers or calf-length skirts. However, the locals were remarkably tolerant of us: they knew that we were not married to each other, yet they were friendly and did not gossip either. Our explanation that we were just colleagues was accepted at face value and I was welcomed with open arms.

At the open end of our alley was a government bakery that opened for business at six each morning. It was easy for us to buy the hot, steaming loaves and rush back down the alley to throw the loaves down onto the kitchen table to cool, before shaking our burning fingers. However, we only bought five loaves at a time. Members of large families would buy up to 20 or 30 loaves at a time and as their combined heat would be insufferable during a walk home, the loaves would be lined up along the roadside to cool.

The basic principles of hygiene never seemed to occur to the Syrians much: on the footpath or on the road, where not five minutes earlier a donkey passed, the loaves of bread would be spread out to cool. However, my arrival in the district gave the locals a new opportunity.

Opposite the entry to our alley was one of the five neighbourhood mosques. Its entrance was not flush with the lane; it was set back just enough to allow space to park one or two cars and I parked my Range Rover in front of the mosque each night. From six each morning the car served as the local bread cooler. It was moderately more hygienic than the street and one did not have to crouch down to turn the loaves over.

Of course, I did not mind my car being used to cool bread. My only complaint was that my side mirrors kept getting dislodged and I needed them to be accurate in order to be able to reverse out of that narrow street. (Being an old car, the mirrors had to be manually adjusted.) So eventually I asked a Syrian friend to write me a large sign for my windscreen, welcoming the bread purchasers but requesting that the mirrors not be touched. I never had to adjust the mirrors again.

Before my arrival the student already living there had made friends with one of the local families. The oldest son was called Mohammad, a name carried by approximately 50 per cent of the local male population. (A local joke suggested that if you went to the Aleppo souk and yelled 'Mohammad', half the men would reply. 'Ahmed' would generate a response from the other half.) Mohammad was about 23 years old and was not yet married. He often dropped by to see us and even if I was alone, I would ask him in for a cup of tea. I drove him to university a couple of times.

Then suddenly he stopped coming around so often. Once or twice he knocked on the door and, on finding that I was alone, said he would come back later when my housemate was home. His behaviour seemed totally irrational. When I finally questioned my housemate about it, he said;

'Mohammad has decided that he's in love with you. Therefore, he can no longer spend any time alone with you. In his mind, it is not right.'

Mohammad came from a family where marriages were arranged and courtship just did not take place. Therefore, his only hope of marrying me was to engage his mother and sisters to the task of winning me over.

A few days later Mohammad knocked on the door. When I opened it, I immediately informed him that I was alone, so as not to embarrass him. However, all he wanted to do was to hand me an invitation to a wedding for the following week. The invitation was an embossed card, rather more elaborate than that normally used in Europe, depicting a shapely bride in a flowing white dress surrounded by pretty pink and blue flowers laced in gold. On the back of the similarly styled envelope Mohammad had written instructions for me in English: '5.30 wenseday wik next I me you take you go my house sisters.' Although difficult to understand I got the general idea. Accordingly, at 5.30 the following Wednesday evening I waited for Mohammad, having dressed in the most lavish fashion I could, while trying to maintain a suitable modesty. I wore a stylish long-sleeved shirt, a long pair of loose culottes that looked like a skirt, skin-coloured pantyhose and high heeled shoes. I also wore my most expensive jewellery and put a ribbon in my hair.

Mohammad escorted me the 150 metres to his own house, where his two sisters and mother awaited me. Their house was similar to ours in that you also entered a courtyard from which various doors led off to unseen rooms. However, the main reception area was upstairs and on a considerably more lavish scale than our own place. Some dozen heavy chairs were lined along the two long walls, while a large china cabinet stood proudly at one end. The chairs were brocaded and covered in plastic, so I crinkled as I sat down. Small tables had been carefully placed in front of every other chair and the floor was covered with a Persian rug.

Mohammad's brothers looked in on me and mumbled 'hellos' before retiring to another reception room next door, from which I could hear a television blaring. His sisters sat down closely, one each side of me, their eyes shining bright with smiles while we attempted some sort of conversation in a combination of my very limited Arabic punctuated with Mohammad's attempts to translate in his equally inept English.

I eventually gathered that we had to go to the hairdressers so, after the sisters covered themselves in black, the three of us left the house for a 10-minute walk through dark, narrow alleys. I need not have been scared, as one of the sisters insisted on holding my hand along the route.

We eventually arrived at a door and knocked. A very small boy with large, frightened eyes peered out through a crack and, seeing only three women, opened the door to admit us. We crossed a dark, dingy courtyard and mounted a couple of steps to a small room lit by a kerosene lamp and some candles. There were already several women in the room, including one dressed in a nightie who, armed with a mouth full of clips and a can of hair spray, was gathering the hair of another into an elaborate arrangement on the top of her head.

I sat down and allowed the conversation about me to flow, enjoying the exertions of the hairdresser with the spray and pins. I was offered several sweets from a gooey plate and asked to hold an abaya of one of the women.

The girl whose turn immediately preceded our own was quite young, not more than 20, and could have, in my mind, cleaned up an international beauty pageant. Her face was strikingly beautiful - I couldn't keep my eyes off her - and she had thick thick golden blond hair. When I saw her later in the evening in all her finery I was convinced of her supreme beauty. She sported a figure-hugging backless sky-blue dress with a long slit reaching her thighs. At the moment, she was just wearing a black coat. The hairdresser spent some time on her, intricately weaving strands of hair into a sort of net that cascaded down her back. The girl was already married and had a bright, cheery personality. After her hair was done she stayed to give advice on how to best fix mine.

When my own was completed, I was barely recognisable. With the considerable help of approximately one kilogram of spray, my hair had been pushed up into a point on top of my head, not totally unlike Marge in The Simpsons. From there it was curled, with strands wisping down onto my shoulders. (To go forward in time, no amount of brushing the following day could return it to its usual flat self. I kept the 'Aleppian' hairstyle for about three days).

While my hair was getting shoved around, there was a commotion at the front door and all the women gasped and rushed around to close the shutters on the windows of the room. I just caught a glimpse of a man walking by the room to another part of the house, presumably the hairdresser's husband, who mustn't catch sight of any of his wife's customers.

Mohammad's sisters and my imagined beauty queen donned their black face coverings once again and we ventured back home through the dark night. As we were now four, we walked in twos, once again holding hands. We left the other girl at her home with murmurs of 'see you later'.

Mohammad was suitably complimentary on our return. We repaired once again to the reception room, where his mother served us bottles of fizzy drink and huge slices of cake. I ate the cake slowly in order to pass a little more time, as it appeared that we were settled in the room for a considerable period of time and no-one was saying very much. Most of my memorised Arabic sentences had already been repeated some half dozen times and I felt I would put my hosts to sleep if I opened my mouth again, unless it was to stuff some more cake inside.

One of Mohammad's sisters left the room for a while, returning in a lavish gown and carrying a frilly shirt, a short, brocaded waistcoat and a thick blood red skirt. She indicated that I was to put these on.

What could I do? Mohammad was still in the room, so I could not disrobe. It was decided that I put the borrowed clothes on top of my own. I felt that I looked like a little fat sausage when I'd finished, and I found it difficult to mentally count the layers I had on. As a finishing touch, the sister left the room again, only to return with a pair of black stockings. They were the self-stay types that didn't need a belt and these were simply put on over the top of my beige pantyhose. It took a lot of effort to get them on while keeping my legs covered from prying eyes, as it obviously didn't occur to Mohammad to leave the room.

After another eternity we finally got up to leave. We were to go to the bride's house which was on the other side of town so the sisters, several other neighbours and I all piled into my car. Mohammad remained at home with his mother. I had thought that he would be coming with us - after all, he'd invited me himself, but he cheerfully sent me away in the capable care of his sisters.

When we arrived at the house, we found a conglomeration of some 30 women all giggling and plastering makeup all over their faces. The bride was about 18 years old, a rather plump and slightly pimply girl, who was wearing a strapless pink taffeta dress. She sat on a sofa looking slightly bored while everyone around her chattered excitedly with each other. We were introduced in a 'by the way' fashion, after which I sat down opposite her, as indicated, and tried to blend into the background. It hardly worked, as people kept asking me all the same questions about where I was from, was I married, how many brothers and sisters did I have, what was I doing in Syria, where did I live, how long was I here, did I like it? A scratchy record was played and some of the women danced together in the middle of the room. The bride also got up and waggled her hips in a lacklustre fashion for a few moments as well, while everyone else clapped and yelled and made trilling noises with their tongues.

Finally, I was forced up as well and everyone stood or sat back and encouraged my solo act. I felt totally silly as I had not yet mastered the art of Arabic dancing and it felt awkward to keep waving my hands wildly somewhere in the air over my head, particularly in a fully lighted living room.

There was a slight commotion at the door with the entry of some new guests. One of Mohammad's sisters rushed over to me excitedly in order to tell me that another European woman had arrived, a woman married to a Syrian man. I breathed a sigh of relief, thinking that I would finally be able to learn what was actually going on.

The woman certainly looked European. She was wearing very tight grey trousers and a plain shirt hanging loose. Her hair and makeup had been kept to a minimum and her only concession to the event was several kilograms of heavy gold jewellery. She sat down next to me and introduced herself, saying that she was from Yugoslavia. Further questioning revealed that between us we spoke smatterings of seven languages, but that our most common one was

Arabic. After our mutual attempts to make ourselves comprehensible in, amongst others, Italian, Serbo-Croatian and Russian, we gave it up. I returned to my careful observations of the room while she chatted to her friends.

She had known one word in English and French, though, proudly patting her stomach as she mouthed the word 'bebe' to me.

A plateful of sweets was handed around and I politely took one, only to have another three thrust into my retreating hands. While I was trying to consume one of them, my fingers still sticky from the wrapper that had, like magic, torn into a dozen bits when I had pulled it, another woman offered me a handful of sunflower seeds. When I tried to refuse, she began pushing them at me, her movements synchronising well with my jaw as I tried frantically to chew up and swallow the candy in order to talk to her properly. Eventually I gave it up and accepted the seeds, several of which immediately attached themselves to the bits of candy wrapper still stuck to my fingers.

Sunflower seeds after candy is not a recommended culinary experience. After a couple I surreptitiously placed the seeds in one of my pockets and managed to dispose of my bits of rubbish and empty seed casings into a nearby ashtray. No-one took any notice of me, as it seemed there were some more noises emanating from outside and several women were peering through the windows. They couldn't actually see much of the road as a high stone wall and several spindly trees stood in the way, but it was obvious that something was out there. In a flash, the women began tossing black abayas around. Suddenly the door burst open to the sound of the trilling tongues and a flood of black cascaded into the room, women of all shapes, sizes and ages, judging from what little of each of their faces I could see. Carried in their midst, like a small boat tossing in a stormy sea, was, of all things, a man.

Something of a passage between the women was created and he pushed his way through, a young man in his mid-20s. He was dressed in a charcoal tweed suit, white shirt and black tie, his thick moustache and black hair carefully groomed. In contrast to the bride he was quite slim. He went up to the bride, who was still sitting serenely in her pink dress, and sat down next to her. The women around continued their trilling chortle and a couple of them, still in black, danced in front of the couple.

Sometime after midnight we all left the house, the women safely dressed in black, to join a group of about a dozen young men who were all hanging around in the street outside. They had all had a good look at my car and I found one lad, obviously feeling ill, asleep in the back seat. The women all piled into the cars, including my own, and we revved up our motors, horns blaring, and launched into a race through the, until that moment, quiet residential suburb. Not knowing exactly where I was going, I simply followed the line of cars, honking the horn amidst the excited cries of my passengers. The groaning gentleman in the back was the only exception. He was being held up by one of the women crowded next to him.

At one stage we drove past a building I recognised: a European friend lived there. So, I laid my hand heavily on the horn while skidding around the corner to catch up with the car in front.

Around and around the citadel we drove, eventually stopping outside a hammam - a bath house - on the corner of the lane where I lived. Two of the women helped the groaning man out of the car, where he was taken into care by some of his waiting friends. With one of Mohammad's sisters, I drove my car back to its spot by the mosque and hand-in-hand we strolled back up to the hammam.

At the entrance all the young men were milling around, not really doing or saying very much. This was their stag party, but their approach to their religion precluded the consumption of alcohol (under other circumstances I would have suspected the sick young man of being drunk, but in fact he hadn't been). Without alcohol, it seemed that the normal sorts of hi-jinks that would take place at a stag party did not occur. The men simply leaned against their cars or motorbikes and casually greeted us with a quiet 'hello' as we walked through their midst. They reserved a special stare for me, though. I was the only face they could actually see, to say nothing of my hair.

Due to my having gone to park the car, we were about the last to arrive at the wedding party. As we climbed the stairs towards the upper level of the hammam, the sound of live music wafted towards me, as did the incredible sounds of laughing and clapping and dancing feet. At the top of the stairs, we turned into a huge space, like a theatre, packed to the brim with the most colourful array of women I'd ever seen. There were over 300 women there, all dressed stunningly in designer-type fashions the like I'd never seen off the Parisian catwalks. They would have been mostly homemade and they revealed huge expanses of flesh through backless dresses, thigh-high splits, ample bosoms teetering on the edge of exposure, bare arms and short short mini-skirts. Every colour imaginable was present and the totality was sparkling with literally hundreds of thousands of dollars' worth of jewellery.

We worked our way down onto the stage where a three-piece all-women band was strumming away. Sitting on a rostrum all alone, in full view of the whole company, was the bride, still in her pink dress. However, as we climbed the stairs towards the stage, the bride descended and disappeared into one of the side rooms.

We joined 'our' group of women at the back of the stage, from where I had a wonderful view of all the guests in their finery as they gyrated in the aisles in front of me. The music permeated throughout the hall and, while it seemed that women could climb at will onto the stage to dance, many opted to remain by the rows of seats in the 'audience' and dance there, some bouncing up and down on their seats.

The bride soon returned and she had changed her attire. The new dress was baby blue and had a split cut so high in the leg that the tops of her stockings could be seen. It was a rather tight affair that hugged her ample curves and she had trouble sitting down in it. This she did, however, returning to her rostrum in silence, accepting the stares of everyone around her.

I found myself sitting with two teenagers who kept up a constant barrage of questions and comments that I couldn't answer. They also had a huge store of sunflower seeds and watermelon seeds, so we sat and munched, tossing the carcasses onto the floor.

At about 2a.m. the bride dismounted the rostrum again, only to mount once more a few minutes later in a new outfit, this time in black and gold. She accepted the cheers and claps and then disappeared, staying out of the hall for about 45 minutes. During this time the women simply continued to chatter and dance and crack seeds. No other refreshments were forthcoming: I'd eaten nothing since lunch but some candy, seeds and a piece of cake and wondered what it was all doing to my insides.

Mohammad's sisters had disappeared with the bride, so I stayed with the teenagers and tried to stay awake. Perhaps a dance or two might have helped, but I had no inclination, and fortunately no-one suggested it to me.

At a quarter to three the bride finally returned, this time resplendent in a European-type white wedding dress complete with a long veil. It was very frilly and fussy and, like all brides, helped her to look quite beautiful. For the final time she climbed the rostrum and all the women trilled their tongues.

With sudden finality some quarter of an hour later, all the colour and gaiety of the room was turned off as if with a switch. From my vantage point on the stage, it was as if I had suddenly gone blind and total blackness had come. One minute the women were dancing in all colours of the rainbow, and the next, they had totally covered themselves in black. Mohammad's sisters, who had returned to my side, followed suit as did all the women around me. Within 30 seconds the only two women unveiled were the bride and me. Even the Yugoslavian woman had covered her head. I could just see her out of the corner of my eye.

The groom arrived with a small contingent of people that I immediately guessed were his two brothers, his parents and several sisters. His mother had a chiffon scarf on her head and his sisters were dressed brightly, if modestly. They climbed onto the stage and the groom joined his bride on the rostrum.

I had trouble seeing all that was going on, because from the arrival of the groom's family I was fighting a battle with Mohammad's sisters. They were giggling with embarrassment and trying desperately to keep our faces totally sheltered from the view of the intruders. This act comprised the holding up in front of all our persons a huge, thick, shawl. I was equally desperately trying to see over the top of the shawl. As they held the shawl up and me down, I pulled the shawl down and jumped up. I caught enough glimpses during my jumps up to catch what was happening and fortunately his sisters finally gave the fight up and dropped the shawl. They obviously thought I had no shame.

The bride and groom eventually joined the family on our level, but the do was not over. They sat down next to each other, this time half facing us, alongside the groom's parents. His brothers and sisters began dancing in front of the two couples and they were joined by a couple of the women from our party, similarly unveiled, who were obviously close relatives. The bride and groom whispered a little to each other and for some reason that cheered me immensely, as I had wondered how arranged the marriage was and if the two young people knew each other at all. The bride suddenly appeared quite relaxed, probably because the whole affair was almost all over.

I was right. Only a few minutes later, without any further ceremony, the family group left, a black cloak being thrown over the bride as she reached the stairs. Rather slowly, as there were a lot of people to move out of the hall, we made it back to the street and walked the 200 metres to our respective houses. It was 3.30a.m.

I returned the clothes to Mohammad's sisters the following afternoon and took tea with the family. At the same time I had to say goodbye, as I was moving the next day to my own house. They immediately offered me a room with them, insisted that I stay, insisted that I visit them every day. Mohammad would miss me, his sisters cried and I bid a hasty retreat. I never saw Mohammad again.

Taxis

There were advantages and disadvantages to having your own car in Aleppo. It certainly gave you freedom of movement, however living in Selemanieh with a car would have guaranteed ulcerous growth, what with having to cope with ever increasing traffic problems as more cars travelled the roads and trying to find parking spaces each day. Another advantage to having a car was that you did not have to put up with taxi drivers. They were terrible drivers. All the windows would remain permanently open, blasting you with wind; their tinny cassette players rang your ears and the meters never worked. At the end of the trip there were always arguments about the cost of the trip and your temper was always rattled. You couldn't even enjoy the trip, knowing that a fight was inevitable at its conclusion.

However, having a car was also a disadvantage. Where would you find adventure without the need to use taxis? How could you experience a society without a variety of taxi drivers to meet? It is only unfortunate that the few awful ones have left a bitter taste and that the bad memories of their trips have drowned out the good ones because, in retrospect, most taxi drivers were OK. Their cars may have all been falling to bits and their driving licences all seemed to have come from cereal packets, but their personalities were a world apart.

Some were rude, uncommunicative, took you on tiki-tours for the sake of a few extra pounds, charged you outrageous prices and damaged your nerves. One evening with a girlfriend, we pulled up in Selemanieh and the driver refused my proffered (and legitimate) amount. He insisted on more so we just got out and he tried to run us down in reverse as we crossed the road behind him. Another time the driver tried refusing to give me any change from 50 pounds for a 25-pound ride. Yet another driver tried selling me some pots and then tried charging me double, telling me it was 'Harram' (religiously incorrect) that I didn't pay more. A third yelled and abused me, tried grabbing my bag from me and called me a 'jahash' (donkey). Considering that I had already paid five pounds more than that briefly shown on his meter before he turned it off so I wouldn't see the fare, I just yelled some explicative at him and scrambled out of the vehicle.

However, there was also the driver who drove into any shady part of the road he could find on a 39-degree sunny day in order to keep me (and himself) cool, all the drivers that accepted the going rate and the driver who took me home without asking where I lived because he'd picked me up just three days earlier.

Then, there was the taxi driver who one night returned my bag to me.

I had gone shopping with Basel and a niece of his who, at seven years of age, was a perpetual handful. She refused to sit still and at one stage tried tickling the taxi driver who, fortunately, did not notice. In my attempts to control her, I got out of the taxi without my bag. We skipped down the road while Basel paid the driver, and it was just as the car revved up that I noticed my loss. I turned and ran back, yelling.

It was too late. The car disappeared around the corner while Basel sprinted off after it and we stood and waited for about five minutes, until he returned to say the taxi had disappeared. We went to Nabil's bookshop and my questioning resulted in explanations that there was no such thing as a taxi depot; that the police probably could not help; and that in all likelihood I would not see my bag again. However, I stated that I had my passport, driver's licence, a lot of money, credit card and other useless junk one normally carries in a handbag. We decided to stand on the road and hope that he would return.

After five more minutes of this I began to despair. Surely the police were the best bet. What would the guy do with the bag? Even if the money was stolen, surely someone would, one day, hand the bag in somewhere? While we were deliberating, the taxi drove past, its one passenger idly swinging my bag out of the window. It had not even been opened and not one pound had disappeared. I gave the driver 500 pounds ($10 US) and a huge smile in compensation.

Taxis were also a wonderful language classroom. They say that monotonous repetition is the best way to memorise a language and taxi drivers certainly gave me that opportunity. The line of questioning was always the same.

'Where are you from?'

'New Zealand.'

'Oh.'

'You know New Zealand?' A sort of semi nod that could mean anything is the reply. Of course, the 'nod' means he doesn't know, but wants you to think he does.

'Next to Australia. Far from here.'

'How long have you been here?'

'Two years' (or whatever).

'Are you married?'

'Yes'. It is always safer to be married.

'Is your husband here?'

'Yes.' Likewise, it is always safer for the husband, even fictitious, to be around.

'Do you have any children?'

'No.' I've never been able to invent any. An optional question that sometimes pops in at this juncture is 'Why not?' Try finding a suitable response to that!

'Do you like Syria?'

'It is wonderful.'

'Good. What do you do here?'

'I work at ICARDA.'

'Ah, ICARDA.' Silence. I then feel I should elaborate before he starts calculating taxi rates in dollars.

'I'm a student, and I work in the desert.'

'You are an agricultural engineer.'

'Yes, sort of.'

'And your husband?'

'The same thing.'

Some drivers left the conversation there. Others would start asking about salaries and hours of work. Still others would try to persuade you to marry them: I think the husband bit didn't always convince them.

Once I had a driver who couldn't stop complimenting me, and he kept looking at me in the mirror and sighing. He asked me all about marriage and was it fun. I said it was wonderful, wasn't he married? He sighed a no. I told him I was ecstatically happy with my husband, the greatest man in the world (which one isn't as a vision?) He just kept sighing and, obviously quite distracted, handed me far too much change at the journey's end. I couldn't help but feel flattered.

Dinner engagements

Syria was a country of contrasts, of duality. Christians contrasted Moslems, the city contrasted the rural areas. Modernity contrasted traditional values. I never felt the contrasts so much as dinner invitations on two successive evenings. Both household heads were businessmen, both had families and both were Moslem. However, one had obviously been successful in the international financial market (including, in all probability, a certain amount of illegal business dealings), while the other was a traditional feed merchant.

I had been invited to the first home because they were acquaintances of acquaintances and because I spoke French. The second invitation came because I wasn't Arabic and was, therefore, different. These were, again, rather contrasting reasons for the invitations. In fact, the feed merchant's invitation came because I had been conducting some research on the marketing and selling of livestock feed and one particularly nice merchant, a very fat man whose paunch pushed his jalabiya out almost at right angles, insisted on our visiting his home.

On the first evening I went with some friends to the Syrian businessman's house, which was in a wealthy suburb. The walls and floor were of marble, expensive Persian carpets broke the floor patterns and light poured from chandeliers. The salon furniture was Georgian in style and the room was crowded with expensive-looking ornaments and draperies. My gin (imported) and tonic was served in a heavy crystal glass.

The dinner table was made of heavy glass mounted on gold-plated legs. The plates were rimmed in gold and the stem and base of the glasses were gold. Needless to say, the cutlery was gold-plated as well. A servant handed around hors d'oeuvre of caviar, pâté and light vol au vents and champagne was offered. The entrees included salmon quiche and white wine, while the main course was stuffed veal rolls served with red wine. After a choice of desserts ranging from creme caramel to Italian ice cream, accompanied by a dessert wine, petit fours were distributed along with cognac and other liqueurs. It was a sumptuous meal of food I had not seen in Syria before. Most of it had been imported.

The following evening my field assistant, Jihad, and I took a service taxi to the feed merchant's house which was located in an old part of Aleppo. He greeted us at the door and ushered us up three flights of stairs to a room overlooking a courtyard. There were no chairs in the room, just a table with a television and cushions to lean against arranged on long carpets running along the floor against two walls. This was Bedouin-style, so I was used to it. The idea is to lean comfortably on one or two cushions placed at right angles to the wall and bend one leg under you. The other you can leave up or down as you wish, but you cannot straighten your legs, as this is considered rude. The only problem is that after a short time, your knees begin to ache. It is then time to change positions slightly. However, after a couple of hours, almost no position is really comfortable, and you begin to surreptitiously straighten your legs as far as possible without causing offence.

After a short time two other men arrived, possibly brothers or cousins of our host. The five of us sat for about an hour, chatting of this and that, with the monotony broken only by the arrival of some tea. For this the merchant left the room for some 10 seconds, returning with the tray weighed down by the teapot and glasses. An unseen woman had carried it up the stairs and by some unseen signal, indicated her presence so her husband could relieve her of the tray. She did not bring it into the room.

When dinner was ready, we went downstairs to a cordoned-off part of the courtyard where a low table and some plastic-covered stools stood ready. The table was covered in plates of food - hummus, moutabbal (an aubergine dip), stuffed peppers and aubergines, some meat dish (lamb), yoghurt, tomato and cucumber salad, and a couple of other dishes I did not recognise. All of them were swimming in olive oil and I understood our host's paunch. He liberally distributed khobz (bread), broken-off pieces of which we used to pick up food we wished to eat. There were no individual plates: we all helped ourselves from the communal plates on the table. The food was delicious; however the huge quantities of oil quickly filled me up and long after I felt I was going to burst our host was still picking 'choice' bits up for me and placing them on a piece of khobz in front of me.

After everyone had finished eating, we made to move back upstairs to the salon for some more tea. Our host asked if I wished to meet the women and of course I said yes. He led me into the kitchen, where three women in long dresses, their heads covered with scarves, were busy washing dishes and heating milk. They immediately crowded around me, laughing and exclaiming delightedly and the host left us alone.

Two of the women led me into another salon, situated just off the eating area, and invited me to sit down. The seating arrangements were the same as in the salon upstairs, except that in this room there was no television and the carpets appeared rather more worn. Several children gathered around and within five minutes more women and children arrived. Obviously, some of the children had raced out to nearby homes to signal the presence of an ajinabieh (foreigner) in their house.

Soon the whole room was crowded with giggling and chattering women and children, and I found myself in the centre, trying to carry on some sort of conversation that largely concentrated on my marital status (happily married, of course) and my lack of children. I spent some time trying to sort out which children belonged to what woman, which was difficult as if I looked at any particular child, he or she would go red and cower behind its mother's billowing skirt.

One of the women began to feed her infant, popping out a breast through a partly buttoned up dress.

Eventually we moved out into the courtyard where a few fresh plates had been added to the general mess left by the men. To my extreme joy, I was invited to sit and partake of their meal. I protested, trying to explain that I was already bursting after having eaten half an hour earlier with the men, but it did no good. I found myself getting laden down with yet more food, as I obviously needed fattening up. How was I to have children otherwise? Gosh, I was so thin (I wasn't really) my husband couldn't even find me attractive.

A guard in the form of one of the older children was placed at the door of the courtyard by the stair's entrance and the women all took their scarves off their heads, revealing their thick, long, plaited hair. Most had black hair, however some had dyed their hair with red henna. They began eating huge amounts of bread dipped into the oiliest parts of the dishes and alternated between stuffing the mouths of children hanging around and their own mouths. I pulled bits of bread off the round given me and pretended to cover them with food and eat.

Suddenly a cry was heard from the guard. All the women dropped their food and rushed to cover their heads, emitting tiny screams of panic. Our host wandered back in while one of the women, who had got her scarf slightly twisted in her hurry to cover herself, started cowering, her face practically in her lap, her hands shaking slightly as they tied the scarf in place and checked to see if any hair was exposed. Our host said something to the women that I didn't understand and pretended to hit the woman who cowered more, but one or two people were laughing, so I guessed it was a joke. He asked if I was OK and would I stay there for tea or return upstairs. I stayed with the women until Jihad gauged it was time to leave.

Aladdin

Although Selemanieh offered just about everything you needed in the way of goods, I always enjoyed going down to the souk in the old city. This 13th century souk was situated in the earliest inhabited part of Aleppo, making it one of the oldest continuously operating markets in the world. In Arabic, it is called the 'souk medina', in other words, the city market. In fact, it was a huge area, hectares square, approximately ten kilometres of tiny, covered streets under fine vaulted roofs behind Islamic gateways, revealing minuscule shops each some three metres by three metres. Each street or area catered to some specific good such as materials, vegetables, nuts, soap, rope, cleaning equipment, beaten metal gadgets, leather goods, kitchen ware, gold, silver and carpets. The special women's souk featured the most ornate and outrageous wedding dresses and sexy underwear possible in rainbows of pastel colours.

The souk was also the most important site on the tourist trail of Aleppo. There was a new tourist souk with fixed prices (they could still be slightly negotiated) where one could buy copper coffee pots, embroidered tablecloths, inlaid wooden boxes, jewellery, scarves and cushions. These were all available in the main souk area as well, but in the tourist souk the shops were more dispersed with the starting prices much higher. The tourist souk had high wooden ceilings and windows letting in plenty of light. The stalls were more open with ornate wooden carvings. In the main souk area, the only light came from dim electric lights; the stalls were dingy and more closed in and you were expected to bargain for everything.

As the souk was so old, some of the buildings were worth visits in themselves. The Omayyad Mosque was situated at one edge of the souk and dated from the year 715. There was an old mental asylum with dark, tiny concrete cells. If you weren't insane upon entry, you would very quickly be. Fortunately, by the time I arrived in Aleppo it was only opened for occasional interest visits. There was still some light industry, although much of this had moved to larger quarters outside the souk area. One old building still housed an olive oil soap factory, where the soap was prepared and cut in a traditional manner - the congealing soap mix, having been spread over a huge floor space some 30 metres long by three metres wide, was cut with a hand-pulled wooden contraption with blades sticking into the soap. It took four people to cut the soap: two people to pull the blades through, one to stand on the blades to steady them and provide enough force to cut through the soap, and one to direct the blades in a straight line. Once hardened, the soap was sold, without further ceremony or coverings, in various shops along the soap market street.

There were also the caravanserais. These were huge inner courtyards with heavy gates that could be shut at night. In the camel caravan days, the gates and courtyards were to protect the caravans at night from thieves and bandits roaming the wilderness outside. Aleppo was much smaller and quite dangerous in those days (although not as dangerous as today, I expect). When I was there, the gates tended to remain open, and the courtyards were full of shops as well. The French Consulate used to have its offices inside one of the caravanserais, not for protection, rather for the historical and central setting.

The souk was made up of hundreds of tiny streets which were not closed to any sort of traffic, except that most motorised vehicles couldn't gain access as the roads were far too narrow and occasionally there were stairs as well. However, there were often congestions in the outer streets as various three-wheeled vehicles and tiny Japanese models tried to penetrate the deepest possible before off-loading or on-loading goods. Otherwise, goods were transported on the backs of motorbikes, bicycles and, of course, donkeys and horses. The latter were also used by itinerant traders to ply goods up and down the larger thoroughfares. Some of the smaller streets ended with a few stairs or a steel rod cutting the access in two. These could be passed on foot but prevented all but the most persistent bicycle or motorbike owners from using them.

The roofs tended to end in domes and there were often decorations hanging down along the route. All the traders were men, nearly all were Moslem and tended to come from the more traditional parts of Aleppo who disdained the 'modern' European forms of dress. In addition, as the souk was the central market for the whole of the north-western part of Syria, most of its shoppers came from outlying villages and towns. Therefore, most men were dressed in jalabiyas, often with red and/or white scarves covering their heads and thick, black moustaches screening part of their faces, and the women wore long dresses. Their heads, and often their faces, were covered in black.

The ensemble provided a lively and colourful place to explore. The house I lived in during my first month in Syria was just a five-minute walk from the souk's main entrance, so I quickly became familiar with its streets. After moving to Selemanieh I was still only a half hour by foot and 10 minutes away by taxi. Thus, I frequently visited the souk to both shop and to chat to the merchants who would always offer cups of tea and coffee in return for a 10-minute visit to while away some of their long days. For me, it was an opportunity to practice Arabic.

In the early days of my time in Syria, tourism was still taking its first few hesitant steps, like a frightened infant. It was easy to spend the whole day in the souk and not meet any other foreigners. After problems began in Egypt, and Algeria became a non-starter for tourism, and as Syria's beauty and friendliness became better known, things started to change.

Now, of course, the souk is gone. It was destroyed in September 2012. Up to 1000 shops, centuries of history and colourful trading are now nothing but rubble.

I meet a new friend

'HELLO, HOW ARE YOU?'

On my second visit to the souk this call, in English, took me by surprise. I turned towards the originator of the call and saw a young man dressed European style - a white T-shirt and jeans - standing behind a small counter. Red and white and black and white Bedouin scarves were piled high on the shelves behind him. He had no moustache. However, it appeared that he had not shaved that morning either. As he caught my eye he smiled. 'Sit down, sit here, would you like some tea?'

As this visit to the souk had not been undertaken with the intention of purchasing anything, rather to meet some Syrians, I accepted with pleasure. The young man called over a boy, who ran off to find some tea.

'How are you? What is your name?'

I told him and asked his own.

'Aladdin. Do you know this?' he asked, scrunching his face slightly as he twirled the strange words around his mouth before tossing them out. 'She sells she sells by the seashore.'

'You mean she sells seashells.'

'Yes, I know. I know another in German.' He rattled it off. 'Do you know any others?' he asked.

I recited how much wood woodchucks could have chucked, and he tried copying me. Then he took a piece of paper and asked me to repeat it so he could transliterate it into Arabic. I offered to transliterate it myself, and my efforts at producing a readable version in Arabic amused both him and another man who joined us at that moment.

'This is my brother,' Aladdin introduced. 'One of nine brothers.'

'Nine!' I exclaimed.

'Yes. We are like a football team. And three sisters. Where you from?'

'New Zealand.'

'New Zealand! Kiwi! I have a name from New Zealand. Wait a minute.' He disappeared behind the counter, reappearing with a large notebook half full of addresses in various different languages. He found the name of an inhabitant from Nelson. 'Can you write your name?'

I did so, giving my New Zealand address. 'But you know,' I said, 'I live here.'

'Here! In Aleppo? Why?'

'Why? I like it.'

'Thank you, but why? What are you doing?'

I told him about my studies and my work. It was the first of many visits. Each time I went to the souk after that, I ended up having tea in Aladdin's shop, or his cave, as he liked to call it. His shop was always full of people, usually his brothers and friends, and as time wore on, more and more tourists as well. He used to talk a lot about himself. He had married about six months before I met him - he was only 20 - and his wife was pregnant, and in due course he officially became 'Abu Mohammad' (the father of Mohammad).

In those early days in Aleppo, I posed as a married woman, thus avoiding unwelcome offers out. Aladdin never asked me out then, however he did want me to come and have dinner at his home and meet his wife and baby boy. A friend of mine from Europe arrived in Syria on holiday, so I asked him to pose as my husband and we spent a very pleasant evening at Aladdin's house. He had asked us to bring a bottle of wine, but when we arrived, he told us to keep it hidden in its bag.

'Don't let my wife see it.'

His wife was very attractive and, although she covered her head with a white scarf, had been to university and spoke better English than Aladdin. She served a wonderful array of food from roasted chicken to kibbeh (a mixture of cracked wheat and lamb), followed by peppers and courgettes stuffed with rice and meat. We cooed over Mohammad, who remained asleep the whole evening, and joked and chatted for several hours. It was only when his wife had returned to the kitchen to clear up that Aladdin asked us to open the bottle of wine. He poured us each a glass, recorked the bottle, put it back in the bag and downed his glass in two gulps.

'Quickly, quickly, drink your wine, before my wife gets back.'

It was the first time he had ever tasted wine, he said, although he had drunk beer before. However, his wife was totally against alcohol.

'I didn't realise, Aladdin. We should not have brought the wine.'

'Don't worry, don't worry. But you will have to take it away with you again.'

So, we found ourselves leaving his house with a half empty bottle of wine.

A few months later I left Syria. I gave Aladdin a photograph of myself before leaving - he had a drawer full of photos from many of his customers - and did not see him for about six months, after I returned and started living in Selemanieh.

My return

THE DAY I RETURNED to the souk I entered through the wool and cotton street. Nothing seemed to have changed. The men were still beating fleeces with their thin, metallic rods and further on innumerable leather belts were still being cut out and stitched into shape. Men looked up as I passed but made no comment. There were just a few boys who smiled and called out 'Hello'. At the end of the street was a stall operated by one of Aladdin's brothers, who smiled widely on recognising me. I smiled back and shook his hand, exchanging greetings and questions on our respective health in Arabic. He offered tea, but I said I was on my way to see Aladdin and where was his shop now? He gave directions and once again expressed his pleasure on seeing me again. I entered the souk's main street.

Changes here were noticeable. There were many more stalls catering to the tourist trade, although fortunately the goods were still restricted to scarves and Syrian clothes. Many of the stall keepers called out to me in English while exhibiting their merchandise. However, the worst shock was the tourists. The street was full of them and many were dressed in shorts. Some of the women had sleeveless tops on as well. I passed two more stalls operated by brothers. One was engaged in a sale; however he still looked up, smiling, and shook my hand. The other simply deserted his stall and joined us, chatting away to me in Arabic. As we arrived at Aladdin's stall, I saw two other tourists sitting drinking tea, with a third examining several scarves. Two more brothers were also in the stall. Aladdin looked up and saw me. His eyes rolled heavenwards, and he half turned, as if to look behind him.

'Oh my goodness. Oh my God. You are here. I don't believe it.'

'Hello,' I piped in.

'Hello. That's all you can say. Hello. One month you have been here. One month you have been in Syria. Yes, I know. I know you have been here and yet you don't come to see me. I don't believe it. My God. Sit down, sit down. Do you want some tea?' He brushed a scarf off a stool and arranged it for me.

He looked tired. His eyes seemed heavy, and his smile was not as jovial as in the past. However, he started asking about what I had been doing and in turn recounted his recent trip to Europe.

'You know I divorce my wife.'

'No,' I exclaimed. 'You haven't, have you?'

'Not the papers. But I want to divorce her. She is no good. She went away for months and just now she has come back. But she is no good, believe me. I want to divorce her.'

'But she is lovely. You don't want to divorce her.'

'Believe me, I do. My wife, my wife. pfff.' Aladdin swept the air with his hand, as if brushing away a horde of flies.

'But how is Mohammed now?'

Aladdin's face brightened and he smiled, an old, long-forgotten smile. 'He is good.'

'He must be 18 months now.'

'Yes, you are right. Just one minute, please.' He got up and went to serve a customer. One of Aladdin's brothers, Abu Noora, came over. 'How are you?' he asked.

Abu Noora was 33 years old and had been working in the souk since he was eight. He never went to school and was unable to read or write. His English was not as good as that of his younger brothers, however he spoke enough to communicate with tourists and had added reasonable Italian to his Curriculum vitae. He was called Abu Noora (father of Noora) partly as a joke because all five of his children were girls. He told me his wife was expecting their sixth child.

'We got married and after one month she was pregnant,' he laughed. 'Pregnant two months! No, that is just a joke. Pregnant after one month.' He took out a much-handled photograph showing a very serious-looking man surrounded by five dark serious-looking girls aged from nine to one. Their mother was not in the photo, so I asked why.

'She very angry, not like her photo. So no photo of her.'

The tourists left and another man simpered into the stall. He was plump and balding, with beads of sweat covering his pate. His mouth puckered a little, as if several teeth were missing. He limply waved his hand in Aladdin's direction and minced towards Abu Noora who, turning around, stood up and put his arm around the man, kissing him on his head.

'My girlfriend,' Abu Noora introduced to me.

'Boy George,' the man tossed back.

'You know about Boy George?' Abu Noora asked me. I nodded affirmative. 'We call him Boy George because he is a she.' he turned back to the man. 'You are a girl!'

The man giggled.

'He is a gay. You know what that means?' I looked at the man again and questions did enter my mind. An obvious gay in Syria! Aladdin returned towards me and whispered.

'He may be a man, but he has no machinery. You know what I mean? No machinery.'

The man giggled again. 'They don't know what they are saying. They don't know what the word gay means. Don't mind them.'

'Your English is very good,' I commented.

'I have lived three years in Canada and two weeks in Switzerland. I still have friends there. I write to them all the time. They send me chocolate and peanut butter. Once a month from Switzerland! Peanut butter!'

'But you can get peanut butter here,' I said.

'Yes, but it is not good. These people,' he idly waved his hand towards Aladdin and his brothers. 'These people don't know what peanut butter really is. That is why I have it sent to me.'

Aladdin whispered to me again. 'He eats them for breakfast. The chocolate and peanut butter. That is why he is so soft. Soft like a girl. No, believe me, it's true.' The man giggled again and groaned himself to his feet.

'Well, I must be going now. I will see you here again? If you want anything, anything at all, any help with anything, please let me know.'

'Thank you,' I said. Boy George turned and walked out, his hips swaying slightly, or was it my imagination? It could also have been the swaying kerosene lantern hanging from the shop ceiling.

Syria's 'secret' police

ANOTHER DAY, ANOTHER visit. I'd met Aladdin part way up the souk street. He was amazed to see me again so soon and his smile lighted up his face. Forgetting whatever errand he had been going to accomplish, he turned around and walked back with me to his shop. The kerosene lantern - presumably refilled - still swung over one of the counters. The electricity was still off. It was August and parts of Aleppo were receiving only a few hours of electricity per day. This, coupled with the nightly water cuts, was causing tempers to rise, but anger was controlled, maintained just below the surface of many of the city's citizens who felt they were powerless to complain or do anything about it. Within the expatriate community, stories were heard daily of whole freezers-full of food being thrown away.

A group of Spanish female tourists passed and Aladdin called out to them in Spanish. They stopped and began examining some of the scarves draped over the counter. During my six-month absence, Aladdin and his brothers had branched out of the plain Bedouin scarf trade into a variety of brightly coloured scarves of different sizes, as well as tablecloths and children's clothing. Aladdin and the two brothers who were present in the shop sprang into action and began pulling out other scarves, both silk and synthetic, for the women's perusal. The women were, for the most part, early middle-aged and most wore shorts. They did not speak directly to any of the brothers, and pulled and dropped scarves on the floor, where they began to get mixed up into a tangled heap. Several came into the shop and within seconds both counters and the floor were covered in scarves. Then one requested an embroidered tablecloth and one of the brothers, Ahmed, pulled out a couple for her to look at. After opening three packs, she selected one.

'I'll take this one,' she said.

'Six hundred.'

'Four hundred'

'Ok, five hundred.'

'No, four hundred, and no more.'

'I cannot. Five hundred.'

'I will not pay more than four hundred.'

'I lose my job.'

'Four hundred, maximum price. If you want to sell it, four hundred.'

'I lose my job.' I laughed inwardly. The little liar! It would be difficult to lose one's job when one's family owned the shop. 'Five hundred. Otherwise, no sell. I lose my job.'

'Ok, five hundred. Will you take dollars? Ten dollars?'

'Yes, OK.'

She handed over the ten dollars and collected the tablecloth. As she was leaving, Ahmed dropped a polyester scarf around her neck. 'A present,' he said.

I decided to go and do some shopping. Aladdin caught me trying to leave. 'Where you going?'

'Shopping. I'll come back.'

'You'd better.'

I wandered down to the fruit and vegetable stalls and selected some onions, peaches and beans. At a nut stall I stopped to sample the variety and purchased half a kilo of pistachios. On wandering back up the street I saw that the crowd around Aladdin's shop had not diminished, so I sidestepped into the handicraft souk. There I fell in love with a pair of imitation gold earrings, which I tried on and asked the price. One hundred pounds. However, prior to purchasing, the young man in the shop invited me to join him in a drink. He called a boy over who rushed off to purchase some 'gaseous', in other words bottled cola.

The young man spoke no English so we made do with my crappy Arabic for a while. Then a lone tourist came by, acceptably (to me) dressed in long-sleeved shirt and trousers. She was beautiful and the young man's eyes shone. She, too, seemed taken with the gold earrings and, after selecting a pair, accepted a drink as well. However, she spoke no Arabic and so began a strange conversation with me as interpreter. At each comment the girl made, the young man turned to me, shaking his head slightly, asking 'Shu (what)?' Then he would reply and the girl would ask me, 'What'd he say?' Half the time I would just throw my arms in the air, laugh and yell 'Mabarif (I don't know)'. However, it transpired that the young man offered the girl his hand in marriage. She was flattered, of course, but thought her 'husband' back home would not be too pleased. He suggested divorce (of course). She said it wasn't possible, as she loved her husband. He said she could love him, himself, instead. He was better than her husband. She mentioned that she was leaving Syria in two days' time. He insisted that she return. She promised she would (she loved Syria), but with her 'husband'. No no, he said, without her husband. And so the conversation and argument continued. I finally got up to leave and she did as well. The young man (who was, by the way, according to our conversation prior to this dream girl's arrival, married with two children aged six and one), his eyes idolising this vision of beauty, offered her the earrings as a gift. I pulled out a 100-pound note but his honour was at stake. Slightly reluctantly, he offered me the earrings as well and we parted, he clasping her hand for some 20 seconds as he reiterated his need to have her back soon, divorced and ready to marry him.

After leaving the shop, the girl thanked me and asked if I could possibly help her purchase some boxes, as she was having trouble making herself understood. We entered the shop, shelves resplendent with inlaid wood (and plastic) boxes of varying sizes and shapes. She had admired a strangely shaped six-sided wooden box, but they came in a group of three and she only wanted one. The man behind the counter had said it was not possible to break the group up and had told her the price was 1500 pounds for the three. I asked if it was not possible to purchase just one.

'One moment,' and the man disappeared, a second man appearing a minute later. He was keen to show off his command of the English language, but on opening his mouth, immediately slipped up badly. I don't think he meant to add the negative.

'It is problem when woman is not beautiful,' he said, looking at me.

'Oh, I see,' I replied, slightly haughtily, although I was laughing (slightly nervously, it must be said. How much more damage could my ego take?). 'So you think I'm not beautiful.'

He had, immediately on stating his phrase, realised his mistake and he went sort of reddish, shaking his head and hands anxiously.

'No no, I do not mean that. You, both you two, very beautiful!'

I decided to tease him a bit. 'But you said I wasn't beautiful.'

'No, no, you are, you are!' he cried, trying desperately to repair the situation. I let the matter drop and asked if the girl could buy just one of the boxes.

'No problem.'

'Ah, I understand. It is only a problem when the customer isn't beautiful, but as we are, no problem, is that it?'

'No, no,' He cried again, immediately. Then he hesitated, trying to work out my meaning. 'Yes, yes,' he affirmed, 'Which one you like?'

The girl made her choice, haggled over the price, paid and we left the shop, but not before accepting his offer to try his nargileh - a water pipe emitting waves of tobacco perfumed with apple - which the shop owner had been smoking just outside. I then returned to Aladdin's shop.

A multi-coloured nightmare greeted my eyes. Every space and corner of the shop was piled with multi-coloured scarves, as the tourist group had simply pulled all the scarves out and tossed them away. In the middle of the shambles stood Aladdin, separating two enormous silk scarves that had somehow tied themselves together. His two brothers and a boy were beginning to refold the scarves, so I settled down to help them. All around shops in the souk were closing, as the end-of-the-day customers made final purchases. A beggar girl passed seeking odd sums of money, the tea boy collected glasses and shop fronts were rolled shut. Suddenly the electricity came on and Aladdin blew out the gas lantern.

'Now it comes on,' he whispered to me. 'Now it comes on, when everyone has gone.'

It took us nearly an hour to fold all the scarves, my managing to complete one to their every three. And even then I didn't always do it correctly.

'No, no, no,' cried Aladdin at least twice, pulling a scarf away from me. 'If you don't do the next one properly, you lose your job. And look at how slow you are! It takes you too much time!'

'How much are you paying me?' I asked.

He laughed. 'I'm just joking, you know me. Please, you don't have to do this. Just sit down.'

I continued anyway. When the job was nearly finished, a man in a green uniform sporting a pair of handcuffs wandered into the shop, and Aladdin's two brothers and the boy disappeared. The man and Aladdin kissed each other, and then Aladdin opened a drawer, fisted 100 pounds ($2 US) and surreptitiously passed it across to the man. He turned to me and whispered,

'Syria is the best country in the world. It has the best government, there are no problems, the best people. You know what I mean?'

The man asked in Arabic who I was. He obviously understood no English at all. I replied to his question and while he listened and understood me, he continued to address his questions at Aladdin, although was happy that I respond.

As he left, I got up to leave as well. Before going, I asked why he had been given 100 pounds.

'Because I take US dollars from tourists. It is a bribe; you understand what I mean? There are 10 or 20 people that I have to pay like that. They know I take dollars from tourists.'

'But I know you don't change money.' Aladdin was always very strict about that and had never changed money.

'I know, but sometimes tourists buy things with dollars. You know that. So, I must pay the bribes. Everyone who works with tourists must do this. It is a shit country. That man was secret police, you understand what I mean?'

I thought that the uniform and mannerisms meant that he wasn't as secret as all that and his total lack of any other language other than Arabic rendered him rather less than efficient, however I said nothing.

Things become awkward

TWO DAYS LATER I WAS back in the souk again, this time accompanied by an overseas visitor, and we joined Aladdin for tea. He made no move to try and sell anything, simply establishing that the man was married. He then asked how old he was.

'Fifty-five,' was the answer.

'Ah, so you are too old. Too old for your machinery to function.'

I looked away. Aladdin tapped me lightly on the arm.

'You know, I see you coming with him and I am jealous. You know that.'

'Come on, Aladdin. You know I'm married.'

'I don't know that. You wear a ring, but I don't think you are married. I don't think you are.' Once again Aladdin proved himself to be very astute, but I just reiterated, 'of course I'm married.' The visitor then expressed an interest in scarves and Aladdin's attention was diverted. In the end 10 scarves were chosen - small ones - and I guesstimated a price, according to how much he would charge me, and then added a bit. I had on earlier visits also listened to what Aladdin discussed with his brothers concerning prices.

'How much for all of them,' the visitor asked.

'How much have you got?' Aladdin asked. 'I'll take all your money.' The visitor laughed. 'No, it is just a joke. I'm a joker, you know?' Aladdin said.

'Three thousand,' Abu Noora said.

'Come on,' said I. 'These are small scarves. The big ones are that price.'

'Two thousand five hundred,' Abu Noora dropped.

'No, fifteen hundred,' I said, and it was agreed.

I earn my keep

THE NEXT TIME I WENT to the souk I was alone. However, I hadn't been in Aladdin's shop more than five minutes when I was joined by a crowd of about 15 tourists from France accompanied by a guide, who settled down in one corner of the shop with a cup of tea. The tourists, mostly middle-aged women, began examining some of the scarves and tablecloths and one woman took down some new items, including children's jalabiyas (long smocks). She asked Aladdin how much they were.

'Trois cent livres. Quarante francs,' he replied. However the woman, not expecting him to reply in French, looked at her husband standing nearby.'

'Combien, il dit?'

'Trois cent livres,' I replied and she looked in my direction. I then added, in French, that they were new to the shop and a very good price. In fact, I was surprised at how cheap they were, considering the embroidery around the collar and other fine details.

'Oh, you speak French,' she exclaimed, in French. On ascertaining that I wasn't, in fact, a tourist, she began asking me for help. Others joined her and within a period of about 10 minutes I had sold the equivalent of about US$150. I had also chatted about Syria and some of the wonderful experiences I had had and the tourists finally left 'charmed and happy' with the country. As they moved off, their guide stirred himself, yawned and surreptitiously dangled a hand in Aladdin's direction. He pocketed 600 pounds ($12 US) and then strode off, calling his sheep-like group to follow him to the carpet shop. I turned to Aladdin in mock fury.

'Come on, Aladdin, what about me? That lump did nothing. He just sat there and drank tea. I did all the selling. Where's my cut?'

'You can have a job here. You come every day, I'll pay you.' I laughed.

'Thanks, but I think I'll stick with my research. But it's not on, that that guy should receive money like that for bringing the tourists here. He didn't do anything.'

'Six hundred pounds?' Aladdin exclaimed, laughing. 'What you call it in English? Chicken feed! He doesn't have to bring them here. But they want to see the souk, he passes the shop, he may get something. But he prefers the carpet shop. Ten per cent, he can get. Think, if they sell each tourist a carpet. Then he earns lots of money, the guide.'

'I'm obviously in the wrong business,' I replied.

As I left the shop, Aladdin wrapped up a colourful sleeveless jacket for me. 'That's your baksheesh (bribe),' he said. The jacket could have been sold for 500 to 600 pounds.

Awkwardness ratches up

OVER THE NEXT COUPLE of months I visited the souk a number of times, each time with someone else. I had become known amongst my circle of friends as someone who 'knows' the souk and who could help find the best shops (and prices). The people I became a 'guide' for also included Syrians who, surprisingly, had never dared penetrate the souk's dim and airless streets. For the most part they were Christians, and for many Christians the souk was a Moslem domain, which frightened them. The animosity between the two religions appeared to be much stronger on the Christian side, understandable as they were the minority, however the souk was a place of trade and traders will always look at the colour of your money before anything else. Your sex or religion was not important.

Then one afternoon I arrived at the shop to find an Australian sitting and chatting to Aladdin. We got talking and I learned that he was doing some research on Bedouins and their clothing. He seemed interested in the work ICARDA was doing, so I invited him to ICARDA for the following day and made arrangements to meet him at his hotel.

Aladdin went very quiet and later on, while the Australian was engaged in conversation with another brother, he began to berate me about my invitation.

'Many many times I ask you, but you never want to meet me and now, just like that, you invite this Australian. Why?'

'But Aladdin, he's a scientist, like me. He's coming to ICARDA to use the library. And besides, I've been to your house to dinner. And I told you that I would not meet you outside the souk.'

'But I want to. You know I divorce my wife. We can go out. We can get married.'

'Come on, don't be silly. You don't want to divorce your wife, and marrying me, no, you don't want to. I am 10 years older than you. I'm too old. Now. No more discussion.'

He went very quiet and stopped talking, so I decided to leave.

The next morning, I met the Australian at the Baron Hotel and we caught a local bus to ICARDA. While waiting for the bus, he handed me a letter from Aladdin.

'I had dinner with Aladdin last night and he told me to give you this.'

I glanced at it. 'Have you read it?' I asked. It hadn't been in an envelope.

'Yes. Aladdin showed it to me and asked what I thought of it.'

I laughed. 'What did you say?'

'I said, 'I don't think this is going to work, Aladdin', but he insisted that I pass it on. He didn't write it himself but dictated it to someone else.'

I looked at it again. As a letter, it was a classic. It began with the declaration, 'Your father must have been a thief for he has stolen the stars and put them into your eyes.'

'He is very poetic.'

'Read further.'

'I have thought and thought about it and I am sure that you are the only woman for me. We should go away together and live happily forever. I want to leave this country and we can go anywhere you want.'

'Ah, therein lies the crux of the matter,' I said. 'He wants to leave Syria. I wonder how he would feel if I said that I wanted to stay here?' I continued reading.

'For me age is no problem. I will still love you when you are old and wrinkled like a date.'

'What more can I ask for?' I commented, after I had recovered from a fit of laughing.

The letter continued with various declarations of undying love, before it was signed and the author of the piece - not Aladdin - had added as a postscript;

'Please do not think about age, because Aladdin's heart does not think about age, just the love it has for you.'

'Amen.' I folded the letter up. 'But whatever can I do? I never meant for him to feel this way about me.'

'My impression is that he doesn't. To him, it is all a romantic image.'

'Of course, it is. In reality he would hate to be married to me as I would never conform to his ideal of a docile, subservient wife. It's just that I hate to hurt anyone, and I hope he isn't.'

The letter effectively halted my visits to the souk as I had no wish to cause any further embarrassment to Aladdin. However, some months later I met a friend of his by chance who said the whole incident had blown over and Aladdin had laughed the whole thing away as a joke. I returned to the souk in some relief, where Aladdin greeted me with slightly less exuberance than before, although still his friendly old self and neither the letter nor the incident was ever mentioned again.

Playing bridge

A certain degree of snobbism existed in the Syrian Christian society, and this could be detected through the practice of speaking French. The French left the country at independence in 1946, so normally it was only older people in Syria who still spoke French. The modern foreign language taught in schools was English. However, many Christians had been educated in Catholic convent schools run by French nuns and they tended to prefer speaking French, disdaining Arabic.

As I was fluent in French, I had some French-speaking friends with whom I would sometimes pass an evening or a day at the swimming pool. Aleppo was crowded with pools. They tended to be quite expensive, with entry costing a minimum of US$1.50 a person. The swimming pools enjoyed a profitable trade in the summer, as during the day they catered to swimmers and sun bathers and at night they set up tables around the pools, turning the places into classy restaurants. Many of them had resident bands in the evening with dancing continuing until 3a.m.

The favourite pool of my French-speaking Syrian friends was in Midan, a suburb bordering Selemanieh. It was a small, family-type pool and its owner was very particular as to who he allowed in. Single men on their own would never be admitted, for example, and Moslems were generally discouraged as well. It was not a popular pool as the water, which came straight from a bore, was really cold. However, part of the grounds was covered by vines, lending dappled shade over tables, and the food was fantastic. In addition, on Friday mornings a group of older men converged to play bridge.

The first time I went to the pool, my friends introduced me to its owner. On learning that I knew a little about how to play bridge, he insisted on my joining them one day. I glanced over at the shaded poolside to where a group of shadows were quietly smoking and calling out bids but I didn't dare, at that moment, go over for a closer look. The men were all in their late 60s and, according to my friends, were either retired professionals, or worked in such disciplines as law.

The following week the pool owner berated me as I arrived, as he had expected me the previous morning and had organised a competition. So, the following Friday morning I returned to the pool and watched the men, from a distance, set their table up. Late in the morning, when the friend accompanying me had to leave, I wandered over to watch the proceedings. They were playing in French.

At the end of the hand, they asked if I wanted to play. I said 'sure,' and took the place of a grey-haired man who wandered off to find a drink. I already knew they played the French bidding system called 'cinq majeur' which was not too different to the system I was used to playing, so I had some notion of it. However, I had never actually played in French before.

The man to my right dealt the cards while his partner shuffled the other deck. The dealer collected his cards and passed before I had even had time to finish arranging my hand and calculate its value. I felt myself shaking slightly. 'Un pique,' I announced, and then suddenly realised that a pique was a spade, not a club. 'Sorry, un trèfle,' I changed, panicking slightly. In my confusion I found I couldn't remember the French words.

'What do you want?' The dealer asked me. I apologised and explained that I wasn't used to playing in French.

'We can play in English if you want,' he replied, condescendingly. But I said we could continue in French, being too proud to cede to him.

After my second call of one no trump, my partner bid three no trump, leaving me to play the hand. I started to really shake, and my stomach knotted, as there was no way to make the game. I went down one trick and lost points.

The next two hands went to our opposition. I made a bad lead, and at the end of the hand one of the spectators told me what I should have done. It made me more nervous than ever.

Hand four. My partner dealt and bid one diamond. I had no diamonds at all, but I had six hearts and 19 points out of a total of 40 for the deck). It was one of the nicest hands I had ever had dealt to me, so I jumped to two hearts.

'Deux coeurs?' the man to the left asked me, a large question in his voice. Obviously, he thought that I had no idea what I was talking about. I could have bid one heart.

'Deux coeurs,' I responded forcefully. The man sighed, either in resignation at my good hand or in disbelief at my incompetence, I don't know. Fortunately, my partner decided to believe me.

'Trois coeurs,' he announced.

OK, I thought, this is going to be my hand. But what should I do? I could bid four hearts - that would be game, and it would be easy to get. But as my partner opened the bidding, he had at least 13 points. Together, we had enough for slam, which would give many more points. But I was unsure. Normally, in my system of bidding, one would ask, through a defined system of bidding things you don't really mean, how many aces and kings your partner had. I was unsure if my partner would understand what I was saying. Play it safe with four hearts? I'd be laughed at. Resolutely, I announced six hearts.

When I saw my partner's hand, I knew it would be easy to play. My partner had the Ace, King and Queen of diamonds, as well as some hearts and I held the rest of the points. I took out the opponents' hearts first, but then I made a big mistake by winning the final round of hearts in my own hand. I had no diamonds, and no way to get back to my partner's hand, as he had no more winning cards except the diamonds.

I hesitated and someone behind me, realising the same thing as myself, reminded me that I had to play from my hand. I realised that he realised that I had been stupid, and it made me panic all the more. I could feel perspiration appearing on my forehead. I played the hand out as far as I could, and then led a card I knew I would lose. It would all depend on what was led back. I was lucky: the man, not knowing that I had no diamonds, led one and I made the slam.

I was still feeling totally panicky during the next hand. Bidding went around once, with both my partner and I passing. I looked down at my cards, using them as a sort of shield to hide behind. The man to my right bid and I think I mumbled a pass. A pass was obvious, anyway. I sat, looking at my cards, waiting. Nothing happened.

Some minutes passed. I was waiting for the man to my left to bid, and he seemed to take an age. Finally, I looked up to find everyone staring at me. 'We are waiting,' one said.

'Pass,' I flustered.

'All that just for a pass?' He asked, unbelievingly.

I tried to explain that I thought I had passed, but I just continued to shake. After that I called my bids obviously.

The men were kind. They realised that I felt totally intimidated by their age, experience, language and the large group of spectators. Over the next hour of play I made several mistakes, but nothing that cost anything. I bid three when we only needed two. When asked why, I said I bid on the cards and not on the points. We made four, in fact, so my reason was accepted. But I also made some bad leads that angered my partner. At the end of the session, I felt wrung out and emotionally and physically exhausted.

'How long is it since you've played?' They asked me at the end. I replied several months.

'We play every day,' they said. It explained why, at times, events had flowed so quickly that I couldn't even follow what was going on or what was bid.

The race

In early spring a group of us thought it might be fun to have a race from Tel Hadya into Aleppo. Tel Hadya was the research station where we worked and it was situated about 30 kilometres south of the city. I regularly ran around the farmland surrounding the buildings and one circuit around the border of the station was 14 kilometres. It was much easier to run there than in Aleppo itself. One only rarely saw people running in Aleppo and the constant traffic and consequent air pollution made it fairly unpleasant.

Mahmoud, one of my regular running partners, and I went to Lattakia one weekend as part of our preparation for the Tel Hadya to Aleppo race. An annual run was being held in Lattakia and we thought might be fun to participate in it. It was being held at a nice hotel and included a sort of gala dinner at the conclusion of the day's race.

Lattakia was a rather pleasant city and port on the Mediterranean Sea. It was fairly near the mountain villages that were home to the Alawites. The Syrian President was an Alawi, an obscure Shiite Moslem sect, so many of the senior government posts were also occupied by Alawis. Lattakia and other nearby places had received some good government investment and, therefore, looked better than some other towns in Syria. In fact, it had something of a European feel to it, as it had wide tree-lined streets and outdoor cafes along some of the sidewalks.

As far as tolerance went, the Alawis were much less conservative than other Moslem groups. The women, for example, did not veil themselves, not even head scarves. This lack of conservativeness was probably why such a fun run could profitably be held in Lattakia, as otherwise participation could well have been limited.

We took a bus from Aleppo which went over the Ansariyah mountain range separating Syria's coastal strip with the rest of the country. It was a beautiful drive as it was cooler and greener in the mountains, which receive much more rain than land on either side. When we arrived, we checked into the hotel and registered for the run, which was going to be held late in the afternoon.

Some 200 people participated in the race including about 30 women and girls. The route was a five-kilometre circuit that we were told would be well signposted. It was entirely on roads and these were not cordoned off so a little bit of traffic negotiation was going to be required as well.

A pistol shot started us all off together and a large group of the fittest young men quickly took the lead. I tend to be more of a steady runner, so I started at the even pace that I intended to run most of the race. However, I quickly overtook all the other women in the race except one that I could see running about 50 metres in front of me.

There were lots of people lined up on the sides of the roads and many offered drinks which, given the race was only five kilometres, wasn't really necessary. More amusing were the pickups that kept passing, slowing down and offering us all lifts!

With about a kilometre to go, I began to increase my pace and closed the gap between me and the woman in front. I finally passed her about 500 metres from the finish line and so crossed first of the women's group. There were lots of cheers and congratulations, particularly from Mahmoud who was delighted for me. He had run very well, however had not quite managed to place in the top three.

We cooled down with glasses of water and one of the race officials came up to me to advise that an accusation of cheating had been made against me. It transpired that the girl that I passed shortly before the finish line was convinced that I had had to have cheated, as, according to her, 'I had appeared out of nowhere' so, therefore, I had been picked up by one of the many vehicles driving along offering people lifts and then dropped just behind her so that I could sprint past her and take her victory from her.

For close to the next hour, discussions between the other girl, the race officials, Mahmoud and I went around and around in circles. She would not accept that I had not cheated – why would we have come to Lattakia for the weekend only to cheat in a race, that we were using as a warmup for a much longer race being held in a couple of weeks? No one from any of the pickups was admitting to having picked me up – because no one had! Slowly and finally, we came to the heart of the matter. She wanted first prize. First prize, in addition to a medal and a tracksuit, was a Swiss watch – a Swatch.

As soon as I realised this, I offered her the watch. In fact, I said I didn't want any of the prizes. They were not the reason why I had entered the race. I just didn't want to be thought of as a cheat. All arguments then ceased and we were all free, finally, to go and have showers and change.

The dinner turned out to be a buffet in the hotel's conference area. When Mahmoud and I entered the room, we were invited to sit with a group of young medical students from Aleppo University. When the signal came that the food was ready, there was a wild scramble to the buffet table. We politely hung back to wait our turn, only to find that by the time we got to the table, there was practically nothing left to eat! We picked up a few bits and returned to the medical students who had done much better than us. In fact, they had devised a perfect plan of attack, as each one had selected platefuls of one type of food to share with the whole table. Obviously, they shared with us so we didn't go hungry.

During the prize giving ceremony, I was announced as the winner and received the medal and the tracksuit, which the girl that came second obviously hadn't wanted. She was delighted with the watch and, smilingly, came to congratulate me, all the earlier animosity forgotten.

A week later we began final preparations for the Tel Hadya to Aleppo run. For three days we ate only protein and continued to train quite hard, trying to run 10 kilometres a day. I say 'trying' because by the third day, having lost all the carbohydrates from our bodies, we managed to achieve only a six-kilometre stagger. We felt just awful. Then for the next three days we didn't train and ate mostly carbohydrates to replenish what we'd lost. By race day we felt almost normal again.

Five of us participated in the race and we had some good support crews that provided drinks along the route, which meandered along back roads back to the city rather than along the busy (and dangerous) main road. As we ran through the countryside, little children came running and screaming up to us. Men called out, were we going to Aleppo? Would we like a lift?

By the 15km spot, the two frontrunners were out of sight. The fifth runner had been several hundred metres behind us, however as one of the support cars passed us, we saw him sitting in the back of the car, apparently having given up. Well, no. At about 22 kilometres we saw him get out of the car about half a kilometre ahead of us so I told Mahmoud to go on ahead as I didn't want that guy coming in ahead of him.

At about five kilometres to go I reached the outskirts of Aleppo. Dusk had fallen and it was getting dark, which it does very quickly in Syria. I found a second wind and seeing that cheat still about half a kilometre ahead of me made me mad, so I started to speed up and managed to pass him with a few hundred metres to go.

As I ran towards the entrance to ICARDA's sports club where our social events took place, a stream of people came running out to hold a ribbon across the path and to cheer me on. It was just fantastic. I pushed across the ribbon and stopped. And collapsed. My legs completely gave way under me and I found myself sitting on the ground. I started to laugh. A few minutes later I was helped to my feet and I was OK. One of my colleagues had earlier offered me the use of their bathtub, so after some celebration I went back to their house and had a good long soak.

Walking up the 102 stairs to our apartment later that night was uncomfortable, but nothing to the pain of trying to get down them again the next morning! It had been only a 30km run – would I ever be able to manage a full marathon?

Deaths and a visit

Most days I walked down to the end of the road to catch the bus to work and occasionally I would walk along to the Greek Orthodox Church and wait for it there. The death notices hanging on the gate always fascinated me in a morbid sort of way. Without local newspapers, it was the only way people could learn of the demise of acquaintances. Other people catching the bus at the church used to glance over the notices and generally they knew, or at least had heard of, someone posted up there. Some of the notices had photographs attached, but most of them were simply a cross, followed by the name, date of death and, perhaps, a short obituary. They were not always written in Arabic, either. They were often written in Armenian.

Within the space of about a week, two of my friends lost family. The first death was that of a child, my friend's niece, who had finally given up her struggle against leukaemia. My girlfriend, Mary, took a week off work to help support the family and one evening I went around to the house to offer my condolences.

Both Mary and her sister were dressed in black and were alone. After my murmurs of sympathy, we went onto other subjects while tea was served. After about half an hour, Mary's mother returned from her third daughter's house where she had been helping with the constant stream of visitors. I stood up for the hand shaking and condolences and the mother sat down next to me, pulling over a number of photographs of her granddaughter when she was fit and healthy and when she was sick in bed. I had never met the little girl, who had been eight when she died. She had large black eyes and even through her illness, her cheerful smile shone through. The grandmother kept up a running eulogy on the little girl in Armenian, while Mary translated for me. I glanced again at the photographs. It seemed such a waste of a life.

Mary returned to work several days later, however she continued to dress in black for the next month in memory of her niece. Every time I saw her, I was reminded of the smile of the little girl, who always knew she was going to die.

One day at about the same time I boarded the bus for work to be greeted by a subdued group. The father of one of our friends had had a heart attack the previous afternoon. He had been a prominent citizen locally and was very well-liked. His only child, Gina, was a good friend of mine and I knew how much her parents meant to her.

About a week after the death of her father, a group of friends and I decided to visit Gina and her mother. Their third-floor apartment fronted one of the main roads in Selemanieh. Typically, it had four rooms: two reception rooms and two bedrooms, although one of the reception rooms doubled as the front hall, and both it and one of the bedrooms had no window. There was a long, narrow corridor towards the back of the building where the kitchen and bathroom were situated, with the only outside light coming from the building's stairwell.

The inside of the apartment was very dark and funereal - appropriate to the occasion, I thought. I had visited before, however had not noticed how really dark it was. Perhaps the crowd of people that greeted us as we arrived, all dressed in black as they were, had added weight to the normally dark heavy furniture that graced the apartment. Another thing that struck me was the number of people that were there. A week had passed, yet, according to Gina when she sat down with us, numbers had not diminished. Her aunts, uncles, cousins and other distant relatives continued their constant stream of visits, all day and during much of the night. Neither Gina nor her mother had had a moment's rest.

Gina was an unusual Syrian girl. I had never seen her in a skirt or dress: she only ever seemed to wear trousers or jeans. Her typical office attire was a pair of denim jeans and a white T-shirt, although for more formal occasions she chose brightly coloured blouses devoid of any frills. She always wore plain earrings and a simple necklace as her only ornaments and never used makeup.

On this occasion she was wearing a black skivvy and black trousers. I didn't know it then, but she would wear nothing else for the next six months. Her mother would remain in black for a year.

Gina's mother was sitting with a conglomeration of aunts and uncles in the front parlour that overlooked the street. We pulled chairs into a semi-circle in the back parlour/entrance hall and Gina joined us, telling us in English about how she had been with her father when he suddenly took ill and died of the heart attack. Her mother had not been home at the time, leaving Gina to wait and break the news on her return. A couple of aunts joined us, perhaps due to an interest in the mixed group we represented, as we comprised two Europeans, a Syrian (Layla) and a Moslem girlfriend of ours. It was a measure of Gina's and her father's personalities that Moslems were also coming to pay their respects.

Gina's mother soon joined us with cups of coffee for everyone. During the whole week she and Gina had been constantly running to the kitchen to prepare coffee and tea, serve it, gather up the cups and quickly wash them for the next group of visitors. We chatted in low tones, our eyes straining to make out the features in the faces of those opposite, so dim was the lighting in the room.

After about half an hour Layla made noises to leave. All eyes were turned towards us as we began to make moves. I drained my coffee cup, placed it on its saucer and set it on the table. Through my visits with both the Bedouin and other Syrians, I had learnt by heart the typical thing to say on finishing a meal or a drink. In fact, I had learnt it by example from my super-polite field assistant when eating with the Bedouin. Wanting to show my good manners, in Arabic, to Gina's mother who spoke no English, I accompanied the setting of the coffee cup on the table with the words, 'Daimeh, insh Allah'.

There was a moment of stunned silence, broken only by Layla's hurried words of thank you and I'm sorry about your father/husband. We shook hands with Gina's mother and aunts, kissed and hugged Gina and scooted out the door. The silence just before we left still hadn't fully registered with me.

At the street corner we said our goodbyes and parted, Layla and I heading alone back towards our apartment.

'Do you know what Daimeh, insh Allah means?' She asked me, all of a sudden.

'It means a sort of thank you for the food or drink, doesn't it? Should I have not said it?'

'Well, no you shouldn't have at all. In fact, it means 'we must have this occasion again, if God wills.'

A wave of horror flooded over me. 'No. Oh my God, I didn't mean it that way.'

'No, of course not. And I'm sure Gina and her mother didn't take it that way either. You're a foreigner.'

Certainly, my subsequent visits to their house indicated that there were no hard feelings. I was perhaps also one of the few that saw Gina's mother dressed in anything other than black, when I dropped in on spec one afternoon. She was wearing a floral dress. However, about half an hour after I arrived, she disappeared into her bedroom, only to emerge some minutes later once more encased in black. Tying a black chiffon scarf over her head, she announced that she was going out.

Promptly six months to the day of her father's death, Gina changed back into jeans and white T-shirts. I wondered if she felt self-conscious in any way, asking herself if anyone noticed the change.

I was not in the habit of trying to decipher the death notices pinned at the church entrances, however Layla pointed Gina's father's one out to me as we passed the family church one day. Suddenly I, too, had an acquaintance that had died.

The prison

Having narrowly escaped the experience of a Syrian prison once, I had perhaps become slightly wary of locked doors and closed escape routes. Certainly, keys were always something of a problem. I locked them in my car twice (Mustapha turned out to be a master at gaining entry into locked vehicles) and twice left them in my house in Shahaba. The first time it was as I was going out and one of the neighbours (our landlord and his family were visiting the United States at the time) said the grandmother had a spare key and he would organise for it to be brought to the house for me.

On my return home an hour later, there was a reception committee waiting for me: the grandmother and some six other people. They handed me my own key ring.

'We went inside and found your keys for you,' they informed me. Nothing was private or personal in Syria and they had considered it normal to enter my home without my being there. As they had kindly come to allow me access to my own house, I couldn't do anything but say 'thank you' and certainly not berate them for invasion of privacy! However, the second time I forgot my keys, I camped at a friend's place over the weekend and collected a spare key from work on the Sunday.

One hot afternoon I arrived home exhausted. Layla was preparing to have a shower and go out to work. She taught English at a local institute that had recently opened, offering lessons in the use of computers, English and French. We had a cup of tea together and I then fell asleep in my room.

My bedroom was the converted balcony. The doors opened outwards into the living room and were made of glass which I had covered for privacy with some scarves from Aladdin's shop.

Sometime around 5p.m. Layla had some visitors. I learned this later in the evening, as I didn't hear them arrive. To ensure that my sleep was not disturbed, Layla closed the doors leading to my room. They all left the house at 6p.m.

As the door slammed shut when they left, I woke up and thanked Layla quietly for having done so as I had to get up for a dinner engagement. I grabbed my towel and slippers and pushed on my bedroom doors. No movement. I pushed harder and realised that Layla had locked them from the living room. There was no way I could escape.

I started to panic. One, Layla had just left and may not be home until 10p.m. Two, I had a dinner engagement in an hour. Three, my bladder was starting to send some desperate signals. I rattled the door harder, pushed it, shoved and kicked it. It remained steadfastly shut.

I picked up a brass knife and banged the glass a couple of times before realising that that was a stupid move, so I put it down and looked out of the window. I knew the sloping roof under my window could support my weight - our upstairs neighbour had once climbed out there, from my bedroom window, in order to rescue five liras (US$ 0.10) that had wafted down from her place - but I did not think I could climb over onto the next-door balcony. I tried climbing out and realised that I would probably not be able to get back in again without help (the neighbour had needed help). Then I saw my front door keys on the table. What providence made me, today of all days, put my keys in my room? They generally lay on the table in the living room. And what jailer would allow the keys to freedom to remain in the jail? I grabbed the keys, half climbed out of the window and began to holler, in Arabic, in English, in gibberish as I began to tremble. I could see a woman sitting reading on a balcony, but she remained resolutely glued to her book.

Finally, the people below began yelling back.

'What's wrong?'

'I am in my room. The door is locked. Please, I have the key here. Can you come?'

'What?'

'Room, locked. key, here.'

'Where is Layla?'

'She is not here, she may not come until later.'

'Throw me the key.'

'You know the house? (I didn't know the word for apartment in Arabic). Come to the right, and right. You see the door.'

I threw the keys and one minute later I was released from my cell.

Arranged marriage

One evening I decided to visit Mary, a friend of mine living a couple of streets away. I arrived at the house to find her in a state of excitement, for her sister, Sonia, was getting engaged. I asked who he was.

'Oh, he's the nephew of a friend of my aunt's. He lives in Australia.'

I asked when they had met, but it seemed that they never had. 'But they really are in love with each other,' Mary assured me.

Sonia came home just then, so I took the shocked expression out of my face and congratulated her. She radiated happiness and told me that they would be getting officially engaged the following weekend in Beirut. Her fiancé-to-be would be flying there from Perth, where he lived.

Piecing together the story from what Mary told me, I've decided to write it from the angle of Sonia's fiancé, as in the end Sonia played a fairly minor role in the whole proceedings. With very few poetic additions, this is how the great romance went.

Rouben's story

ROUBEN RETURNED HOME after a hard day in the printing shop, which included two hours of overtime. Besides the daily newspaper, there was a letter from his aunt in Syria. Opening it, he discovered two colour photographs of a woman: one a full length pose and another featuring her face. Her hair was long and dark, and flowed thickly over her shoulders. Her dark eyes and full lips traced the hint of a smile, and her body seemed curved and shapely beneath a yellow dress adorned with gold and puffed-up sleeves. Rouben gazed at the photographs and decided that she had to be the one. She would be his wife.

Turning to the letter, he read that the girl's name was Sonia and that she was 22 years old, had studied English literature at Aleppo University and was currently working as a secretary at the university. She had to be a pleasant girl, Rouben thought, or his aunt would not have sent the photos. It seemed that his aunt was a friend of the sister of the girl's mother. He picked up the photo depicting the girl's face again and found an attractive softness about the features. He decided in the course of the evening to compose a letter. He would get a haircut and his photos taken the following day.

Rouben had been living in Australia for the past seven years, ever since landing as a penniless immigrant tagging along behind a cousin who had landed there three years earlier. He had spoken almost no English and had no qualifications. During his first two years in Australia, he worked on an assembly line during the day and studied English, followed by courses in printing and graphic design, at night. During the following four years he slowly increased his standard of living. He purchased a car and then a small house. One-by-one he acquired those appliances so necessary for a typical Australian family: a television, washing machine, a fridge and a freezer. These items came only slowly, as he abhorred the idea of credit, preferring to buy everything with cash. His house was his only concession, but he ensured his mortgage payments were reimbursed in good time. About a year ago, he decided it was time to find a wife. However, he had no wish to marry an Australian girl. Despite his present Australian nationality, and he felt himself an 'Aussie', he wanted to marry a good girl from his own background. So, he had written to his aunt to try to find him a suitable mate. This was the third set of photographs his aunt had sent him. The first set he had rejected: the girl's face did nothing for him. The second set had been acceptable, but by the time he had replied, it seemed the girl had found herself another suitor. There would be no delay this time.

When Rouben's aunt received her nephew's letter and photos, she arranged for a meeting with the girl's parents. After her visit, Sonia's parents put the proposition before her. They had, of course, been aware that their daughter's images had been sent to Australia: they had supplied the photographs themselves. However, Sonia had not been informed. They handed Rouben's photographs to her.

Sonia looked at the photos. She saw a young man, clean-shaven and not at all unattractive, sporting a suit and sober tie. His thick black hair was newly cut and he seemed pleasant, although his stiff posture bore no trace of a smile. In fact, this thought did not occur to her, as in her experience people did not smile for photographs. The stern, unsmiling look was the fashion.

'Let me think about it,' she told her parents. She felt no anger towards her parents at this attempt to find a husband for her. Although she was Christian and free to meet young men and fall in love in a normal fashion, most Armenians living in Syria dreamt of emigrating. Her parents had grasped at an opportunity to allow their daughter what they thought would be a better life, which would be in a largely Christian society rather than being a minority in a Moslem one. The Armenian society in Syria was a double minority, being both Armenian and Christian, although their nationality was Syrian.

The following day Sonia raked the university library for all the information it contained on Australia. She liked what she read: clean, blue beaches, modern cities, cinemas, shops. In short, Australia offered a bright and happy future. In the first hour of darkness, she walked out of the university, sidestepping litter on the path. She looked at a group of veiled Moslem women, their black scarves totally covering their face, as if seeing them for the first time. She hailed a taxi, an ancient beat-up contraption which honked its way through undisciplined traffic and she argued with the driver about the fare when she reached home. The daily power cut was in effect and she inched her way to the front door by torchlight. It took no effort to accept her parents' proposal. Rouben's aunt was instructed to reply to her nephew and she was handed a couple more photographs of Sonia for good measure.

About a month later she received a letter, written in Armenian, from Rouben. It included several other photographs, on the backs of which he had written, in English, 'the kitchen', 'the living room', 'the garden', 'the street (with my car)'. There were two more photos of Rouben himself, looking more relaxed than the official ones she had seen earlier. He was even smiling. His letter was full of admiration for her figure and face, and it described in detail his house and neighbourhood. Sonia immediately sat down to reply. It was difficult to admire his possessions without seeming mercenary, however she managed to express some liking for his looks and ended with details concerning her work at university and the books she had studied.

Her own letter was quickly replied to, and so began a frequent and passionate correspondence. Each letter Sonia received seemed to burn hotter in her fingers and she felt herself deeply in love. In Australia, Rouben was feeling increasingly anxious. He pinned Sonia's photographs all around the wall of his bedroom and re-read her letters every night.

After about five months, the telephone rang late in the evening at Sonia's house. Her father answered and called Sonia. Breathlessly, her heart fluttering, she answered. Neither of them knew what to say. They were both trying to feel the other's voice, read the other's thoughts. Finally, Rouben said;

'I'm coming to Beirut to see my brother in three weeks' time. Can your family come to Beirut? I'd like us to get engaged.'

Rouben was unable to enter Syria as there was some problem with his not having undertaken his Syrian military service, so the engagement party was held in Lebanon. Sonia, accompanied by Mary, spent some 10 days in Beirut with Rouben's family and their parents joined the group for the official parties. After their return, I was treated to the sight of scores of photographs of the happy couple, on their own or with other people, always in the same pose, Rouben standing slightly behind Sonia with an arm around her. There were several photographs of Rouben with his arms around both Sonia and Mary. He never smiled in any of the photos, however he appeared very pleasant and Sonia was ecstatic. Several months later, her bags packed, she set out for Australia to marriage and her new life.

Shopping in Beirut

My Canadian grandfather used to tell me how fantastic Beirut was. 'The Paris of the East', it was called, and he loved visiting for his work and he would often take my grandmother with him.

In 1975 civil war broke out in Lebanon and over the next 16 years some 150,000 people were killed, over 200,000 were injured and around 20 per cent of the country's population was displaced. The civil war ended in 1990, although Lebanon remained a relatively unsafe place to visit.

When I was living in Syria, the borders with Lebanon were open and I met several people from Lebanon as they passed through Aleppo for work. I was keen to visit Beirut as I had heard so much about the city from my grandfather, so a friend and I decided to spend a long weekend there.

As I was working in Syria, I had to apply for permission to apply for a visa for Lebanon and, once approved, I had to obtain it at the border. For this, we had to travel to Beirut from Damascus rather than Aleppo. We went to the service taxi station in Damascus, from where huge American cars made the trips to either Beirut or Amman in Jordan. Each car could take five passengers and drivers could get quite vicious, trying to be the first to fill their cars so they could leave. It was always best to try to find a car already nearly full and to try to avoid handing your passport over to a driver as you'd then be stuck in his car.

The service taxi station was always an adventure. All the cars would be parked any which way yet somehow, they were always able to disentangle themselves when required to. We looked around for a car that already had three people and couldn't find one. One of the Beirut drivers then nabbed us and, after we explained which part of Beirut we wanted to get to, he said we would be leaving with just four people. I told him that we needed five people, however he insisted that four was enough and that the price would be 300SL each. We confirmed that it would be 600SL for the two of us and climbed aboard.

Just before the Lebanese border I handed him our money and he got all mad and said that we owed him another 300SL for the missing passenger. A huge argument developed, however he eventually subsided and we continued to the border. At the border, they would not let me leave Syria as I had no Lebanese visa in my passport. I explained that the visa was waiting for me at the Lebanese border post, so the driver had to take my passport (without me) to the Lebanese border post, get the visa and return to the Syrian post for me and the stamp allowing me to exit the country.

Given the driver had been pretty good with all the mucking around – I was also thankful that he hadn't just done a runner with my passport, after all – we decided to give him the extra 300SL. However, our driver now said he'd had to pay more for the visa and he'd had to bribe the Syrian police to let him through with my passport. He claimed that he'd had to bribe them with 500SL! So, we ended up having another argument, which is always an interesting thing to have when the person you are arguing with doesn't really speak English, and your Arabic isn't really up to holding a sustained, irrational discussion. However, I knew I had right on my side, as one never bribed Syrian police with 500SL. A bribe might be 10 or 20SL, not much more. Our driver finally raised the white flag. He also accepted the proffered 300SL.

The taxi route took us through part of the Beqaa Valley and over the mountains, still partly covered with snow. The land looked agriculturally rich and there were a lot of houses, however the road and many buildings were in a sorry state, some completely ruined, and others just shells with all the contents, including the windows, either destroyed or looted. There were checkpoints all along the road, however our passports were never requested.

As we reached the suburban parts of Beirut, we saw whole areas completely bombed out. Roofs and floors of multi storied buildings were just lying directly on top of each other. Other buildings had large rocket-sized holes or smaller bullet-sized holes and many many buildings were just shells, with or without a roof. In these areas we couldn't see any glass, nor could we see anything inside any of the buildings either.

Our driver left us in West Beirut about half a kilometre from the guest house where we were to stay. Once we got out of the taxi, we asked someone for directions and he immediately offered to drive us there. This part of West Beirut was quite nice, with nice apartment buildings around and, compared to parts we had driven through, much less damaged.

The only thing waiting for us at the guest house was an envelope with my name on it and inside a key giving access to a couple of bedrooms. The only map that we had of Beirut was 18 years out of date and we really had no idea where to go. We decided to just walk and see where the road took us.

The first shop we came to was a wonderful supermarket full of all sorts of food and goods and plenty of workers who came up to us, smiling and helpful, holding out open paper bags ready to fill with anything we might want. They must have seen my mouth scraping the floor at the sight of so many different sorts of food all gathered together in luxury under one roof, and types of food that I hadn't seen in months. More than 20 years later I still don't know how I managed to get out of the shop without buying anything, although I remember that I thought that if I started, I'd never stop.

We continued walking, without much idea where we were going. Occasionally we saw roadblocks down some streets, so we avoided these. At first, whenever we saw anyone in a military uniform we froze, however after a while we began to relax, even when we saw a rather stern machine-gun toting soldier guarding a closed shopping complex.

Just after we passed him, there was a sudden loud 'bang' as something bounced off a wall next to where we were walking and hit the ground. My overactive imagination went into overdrive as my heart and nerves took fright. It turned out to be a football that another soldier was aimlessly kicking against the wall!

Some more streets and turns later, we found real life. We had hit Hamra Street, West Beirut's shopping area and old Beirut's (pre-1976) fashionable hang-out. People were walking around, hawkers were calling and shops were open. They appeared to offer everything and anything from fashionable clothes to gold watches and books. Books! My nose found Beirut's largest and best-stocked bookshop boasting books in both English and French. Within 30 minutes I had filled my bag, found a more up-to-date map and had had lengthy conversations with several of the staff on where to go and what to do in Beirut.

The strange thing about Hamra Street was that in appearance it was very much like a shopping street in Aleppo – a little dirty, a little rundown with cracked pavements and rubbish strewn about, and with lots of people moving any which way with complete disregard for any traffic. Cars were mis-parked on both sides of the road and there were hawkers and street vendors of all sorts, hanging wares from strings in between streetlights, displaying goods on car bonnets, on the ground or even on bicycles. However, once inside a shop, you were immediately transported to Europe – the goods, the way the shop assistants dressed and the way they spoke was not Middle Eastern at all. In fact, all the shop assistants spoke French and many were women, which you didn't see much in Syria. The women were all dressed European-fashion which, that year, included rather short skirts.

We continued walking towards the sea, stopping briefly at an American-style ice cream parlour where most customers were young and who arrived in cars, leaped out, purchased their sundaes and drove off again.

The cars themselves were rather fun to see. There weren't many new cars in Syria – actually, there weren't many private cars in Syria at all, however Lebanon had a full range, from the typical rundown jalopies to brand new Mercedes and Volvos, many of which would most likely have been stolen from Europe and transported to Lebanon by ship. We passed some car yards where the provenances of the vehicles were even proudly advertised, such as 'from Geneva via Marseille'.

By the time we reached the seaside it was early evening and plenty of people were out strolling along the promenade that ran along the waterfront. There were also lots of hawkers pushing little wooden carts by hand, selling tape cassettes (they were also playing them on tape recorders run off car batteries), nuts, fruit, candy floss and various plastic trinkets. At the roadside were dozens of vans selling drinks (tea, coffee or cold soft drinks), ice creams or even nargileh (water pipes) with little stools to sit on for those wishing to partake.

At the promontory there was a fairground, so we took a ride on the Ferris wheel which gave us a wonderful view over that part of the city. In the distance we could see ruined buildings, however most of the nearby buildings looked pretty good. Across the road was a hamburger joint and we could see patrons being served burgers with side orders of chips and salad and with little paper umbrellas in the drinks. We walked by later and saw that the paper placemats had little jokes printed on them, one of which seemed particularly appropriate for Beirut. 'Who says civilization doesn't evolve? Every generation finds new ways of killing people.'

When we finally alighted from the Ferris wheel, the owner refused any payment. We continued along the waterfront until we came into view of Pigeons' Rock, just off the coast. The sun was setting and there were hundreds of people sitting and standing around waiting for the sunset. Street photographers were in packs, taking instant shots of people for 2000 Lebanese pounds, using the rock as a backdrop. On the other side of the road we could see damaged and decaying buildings which were, never-the-less, being lived in.

We got back to the guest house just after dark and had showers before working out what to do for dinner. According to the map we had, we would be able to find restaurants and exciting nightlife downtown near the hotel district. The booklet I had bought at the bookstore listed a fine selection of restaurants featuring cuisine from all over the world, plus nightclubs and discos. We thought we'd take a taxi and see what we might find.

While we were deciding this, a night watchman turned up. I explained to him what we were thinking of doing and he was a little apprehensive. He strongly advised us to stay nearby and try one of the restaurants either near the guesthouse, or back along the waterfront.

Prudence won out in the end and we ate in a nearby restaurant, including having some very reasonable Lebanese wine. We certainly had fun observing all the clientele. Most were young – our age or younger – and most were speaking French. We could have been in a restaurant in Geneva or Paris. The women were all attractive and wore short skirts or tight trousers and it was impossible to tell whether they were Moslem, Christian or otherwise; they were probably a mixture of all three.

The following morning, we headed out towards Martyrs' Square. We had it in our minds to just walk and look and see, however we somehow managed, by some incredible good luck, to end up walking past all of the 'famous' places in Beirut. By 'famous', I mean all the places that we had seen photographs of in books on Beirut. The first landmark we happened upon was the square where the Statue of Riad Solh stood – or perhaps better known as the bankers' corner with the Arab Bank. The buildings were, of course, wrecks, and down some of the side streets we could see nothing but piles of rubble and roadblocks with armed soldiers patrolling. Down the streets not blocked off by soldiers were sorts of shanty towns, where residents had obviously just rebuilt shelters and shops with the rubble following each explosion. The road was pockmarked and uneven and there were pools of dirty, smelly water.

We risked a quick photograph, returning the camera to a bag hidden under a jumper, and then started to walk down one of the streets. An army vehicle stopped us and the soldiers, in blue camouflage uniform designating Lebanese police, jumped out and asked us who we were, where we were from and did we have any cameras? My shoulder bag didn't have a camera, so I responded negatively and helpfully opened my bag for their perusal. They smiled and waved us on.

We went down one of the 'shanty-town' streets and stopped at a little drink shop for lemon juice drinks. One of the people working in the shop was cleaning and preparing a tea trolley, probably for use in nearby streets later in the day. The trolley was constructed in such a way that it could be pushed around by hand. It had a coal stove built into it with a beautifully ornate, tall tea jug perched on top. The tea could be poured from a tap at the side.

At the end of another street, we could see huge piles of rubble – completely destroyed buildings – and yet another major road block, where cars were being stopped by military police. We knew that Martyrs' Square was in that direction, however we were a little disoriented as to its exact location. In addition, we didn't like the idea of trying to get through the roadblock, as we were unsure of the various factions. While we were deliberating, we noticed a string of people climbing up a ruined staircase into what looked like a church. Most of the people were carrying red flowers. We decided to follow them.

It was a church. The roof no longer existed, although bits of it hung down rather precariously into the church expanse. We did not stand under those bits. The building was also completely empty. There was no front door and the side door hung permanently open on one hinge. At the back was a small room with a staircase leading to what would once have been a gallery – it now led nowhere, and the stairs were mostly wrecked. However, the facades were still quite beautiful in some parts and the marble pillars still stood proudly along the sides of the church. At the altar end was a large hole in the wall – I guess created by a missile or some such weapon. There was a low altar (the original or a recent addition, I don't know) and people were walking up to lay their red flowers on it. Behind the altar stood a priest, resplendent in his full regalia, tall pointed hat, white embroidered robes and an ornate cross. Another priest stood to one side, tuning a flute. As we stood and watched, some people came in with a battery-operated synthesizer. A photographer set up his equipment along with a video camera. More and more people arrived and we managed to mingle, but we had no idea what was going on. Eventually everyone gathered around the altar and started to sing. They were Maronite Christians and they were singing in the original language of Christ (which was only commonly spoken in a place called Maaloula, a small village just north of Damascus in Syria.)

The hymn they were singing seemed so sad and, looking at all the damage and ruins around us, so fitting to the scene. Yet here we were in West Beirut (the Moslem side), in the middle of a church service. And while the tune was sad and haunting, the incomprehensible words (for us) were punctuated with 'Halleluiah'. It seemed to symbolize Beirut: despite agony and suffering, people could still gather in ruins, call it a church and sing praises. An hour or so later we witnessed a similar scene at a Mosque. The Mosque was totally in ruins, so much so that people couldn't even go inside, yet there were crowds and colour and light and praying and laughter.

We went out of the church's side doorway to survey the scene of total destruction all around us. There wasn't a building in sight that was inhabited and there were piles of rubble, rubbish and dead and decaying trees everywhere. Grass and weeds also grew in abundance, signifying that the battles that took place in this area happened some time ago. We could not determine which direction to go to find Martyrs' Square. A man was standing gazing fixedly at the ruins, so we asked if he spoke French. After an affirmative, we asked where to find Martyrs' Square. 'I don't know, I don't know anything anymore,' he replied, looking totally shocked and devoid of colour. 'It's been years since I came here, and I don't recognize anything anymore.' I asked if he had travelled far: where was he from? 'From Beirut', was his reply, however he had never ventured into this part of the city since the bombing and trouble had begun.

As it happened, the destruction we were looking at turned out to be Martyrs' Square, or the Bourj. This was the old centre of the city: the meeting point for everyone and everything. Buses and taxis terminated here; there was the opera, police headquarters, cinema, etc. It had been a large, open, shady square with the old souk extending outwards from all four sides. During the civil war it was also the meeting point between East and West Beirut (and a crossing point) and was the centre of a lot of fighting. The statue that graced the centre of the square, incorporating several figures including a woman holding aloft a torch (not entirely unlike the Statue of Liberty) was still standing, although it was damaged.

Both on top of and around the statue were lots of 'tourists'. They were, for the most part, from Beirut like the gentleman we had spoken to outside the church, who were in the process of rediscovering their own city. Cameras were clicking and children climbed all over the statue, using bullet holes to aid their grip as they climbed up. Near the steps leading to the statue hawkers had set up umbrellas and deck chairs so that people could relax in the shade and drink tea, coffee or cold drinks as they gazed around. Official photographers wandered around taking instant pictures and selling postcards showing the area as it looked 17 years earlier. We bought the postcards and matched photos we'd taken of the same spots. Today, over 20 years later, my collection of postcards and photos showing the 17-year difference remains as heartbreaking as ever, especially as I imagine much of Syria now looks like the Beirut of 1992.

A number of different factions of military groups also appeared to be either stationed at the square or included the area as part of their patrol. We bumped into the Lebanese military police that had earlier stopped us in the street. This time, we hadn't hidden our camera, however they didn't say anything about it to us. In fact, they invited us to take tea with them.

There were several truckloads of Syrian military personnel. They were easy to spot as their vehicles all carried the Syrian flag and photos of the Syrian President. One truck even had posters advertising L&M cigarettes, which was a Syrian brand.

We left the square in the direction of what appeared to be the Beirut tourist route towards the city centre. There was a constant stream of pedestrians like us, or those in cars all following each other along streets piled high with rubble and shells of wrecked buildings, grass and weeds growing everywhere. The roads had been cleared just enough for traffic to pass, however there were pools of water and dirt underfoot. The Emir Mansour Mosque had grass and weeds growing out of its walls and nothing but rubble, rubbish and some sandbags in and around it.

Gradually the desolation gave way to some form of life. It was a sort of shanty-town existence, but things seemed to operate. We purchased some very good ice creams to eat as we walked. Eventually we made it to the waterfront again, emerging from the rubble right opposite St George's yacht club, which, completely incongruously, was full of new and expensive-looking yachts and motorboats in working order. There was a swimming pool with people lounging around it, with the destruction of all the streets around as a backdrop. In fact, the primary backdrop was the St George's Hotel itself which was nothing but a shell with, from what I could see, some military types living inside.

We walked through the hotel district – the district we had been planning to come to for dinner the previous evening – and it was completely empty other than some military patrols and lots of posters of the Syrian President and Iranian Mullahs. We couldn't see any restaurants, so the guidebook I had purchased the previous day was a little out of date.

We promenaded along the waterfront. There were lots of men and boys swimming in natural pools in the rocks or sunbathing or fishing on them. The children laughed and screamed in delight as gentle waves washed over the rocks and it was hard to imagine the hell that they had been born into, to see them so happy. People sat around drinking tea and eating titbits offered by the hawkers. It was all quite relaxing.

As we walked along the waterfront, the destruction of buildings on the other side of the road gradually gave way to buildings that had been repaired and were being lived in and we eventually ended up back in the area we had visited the previous day. We found a Lebanese restaurant near Pigeon's Rock and ordered a large meal of mezzeh (hummus and other dips), shawarma (grilled meat) and farooj (chicken). The waiter was delighted to have foreigners there – the only other customers were some soldiers – and he spoke to us at length in French and suggested things to try, including some fabulous chicken wings in a sort of tartare sauce and the house specialty, kibbeh nayah, which is raw minced lamb mixed with cracked wheat.

That evening, we met up with Lamiya, a colleague that came to work in Aleppo from time to time. She picked us up at 9pm, a normal time to start an evening, with her boyfriend, Assan, who drove us through the checkpoint into East Beirut to his home. The suburb where he lived felt like a quiet suburb almost anywhere in the world, with mostly villas, lawns and trees. Assan's home was immaculate, with chairs that had been richly embroidered by his grandmother. Chandeliers hung from the ceiling and the plaster work on the walls was clean.

However, Assan told us that everything in the house had been repaired – many times. The day following any 'incident', the whole neighbourhood could be seen out repairing, repainting and rebuilding. Sandbags surrounding the house had been erected and dismantled numerous times. As we discussed the impacts of the civil war, both Assan and Lamiya laughed and joked. It was their way of simply accepting or even just trying to blot the whole war out. They said that maybe one day it would really hit them, but for now they were just living.

We drove to Joigny, about 20km north of Beirut, parked and wandered around by foot. This was really like I had imagined Paris of the East. Expensive shop after expensive shop stood like sentries on both sides of the road, with prices higher than in Geneva. There were cinemas, expensive restaurants and seaside resorts and everything looked new, modern and very very expensive. It looked the way parts of Dubai now look.

We then drove up the mountains to a restaurant in an old building with huge windows overlooking the bay. It was fabulous to look down onto Joigny and see lights sparkling onto the

Mediterranean Sea. The restaurant's menu offered crepes of all types and we gorged first on savoury ones, followed by sweet ones, washed down with Lebanese wine. As we ate, Lamiya and Assan entertained us with stories of life in Beirut during the civil war. They laughed and kidded each other and accused each other's factions of causing all the trouble. Lamiya was from West Beirut and was a Moslem Shiite, while Assan, from East Beirut, was a Maronite Christian. Yet, they had been dating for six years and had seen some rough times together. Lamiya would sometimes stay nights in East Beirut when there were border curfews, however restaurants always seemed to stay open so there were always places for them to meet.

Lamiya laughingly apologised for not being able to invite us to her home. Her street was controlled by a faction of fanatic Shiites and it would be too dangerous for us. Assan couldn't visit her home, either.

Before taking the bus back to Aleppo the following day, we returned to Hamra Street for some final shopping, mostly books for me. The bus took us northwards along the coast and I reflected on how incredibly beautiful the country was and how incomprehensible it was that people would want to try to destroy this, simply because some people had a slightly different way of viewing God.

Weekend excursions

Syria was a wonderful place for tourists, providing you didn't expect five-star luxury travel and were keen to experience Middle Eastern culture. The main reason it was so great was that there weren't very many tourists and Syrians were among the friendliest people in the world.

Syria is a relatively small country, so it was easy to travel around and visit some of the fabulous sights on offer. During the three years I lived in Aleppo several friends or family visited and I would often take them on weekend excursions.

One such trip started very early in the morning at the local bus station in Aleppo. The bus station offered an opportunity to view a whole cross-section of Syrian society at one time. There were women in immaculate, glittery outfits with incredibly complicated hairdos held together with kilos of spray and gel and perfectly, if overdone, made-up faces, to women dressed totally in black. The men's attire ranged from shirts and trousers to Bedouins in jalabiyas. Hawkers were everywhere, selling such wares as packets of chewing gum, ice creams, drinks, fruit and cushion covers. Old men and young boys wandered around looking for dirty shoes to clean.

The station building itself was undergoing reconstruction work, so it was dirty, dusty and dimly lit. Each window offered tickets to different places, with the place names written in Arabic over the windows. The window for Hama was easy to find and the tickets cost 25SL (50 cents) each. We returned to the bus, reserved two seats by placing our bags on them, and waited in the relatively cooler outdoors. Nearby, small groups of fellow passengers, mostly men, milled around together with half a dozen girls in their late teens. Two of the girls were in jeans with the remaining four in very clean, pressed and dressy skirts. Some had scarves covering their hair, however they all looked as if they had just come from a beauty parlour.

We began conversing with a group of the young men. None of them spoke much English, however a mixture of Arabic and English sufficed. One of them, a truck driver, was heading to Damascus to fly, the following day, to Brussels. He was picking up a truck there to drive back to Syria.

Eventually people began boarding the bus, as did a group of hawkers who had been standing around waiting for this very moment. Once inside the bus, when everyone was seated and unable to move or turn away, the hawkers would have a captive audience. In addition, the sudden change from the sheltered bus station with its slight breeze into the stuffy, airless bus with its teeming humanity squeezed into every corner could virtually guarantee an increase in interest in purchasing ice creams and drinks.

At the last minute, a Bedouin woman huffed her way to the bus, lugging a huge sack full of wares she had purchased in the souk – articles of clothing, cloth, plastic and metallic kitchen utensils and probably many other items hidden amongst the folds of the monstrous contraption she carried. This she heaved onto the bus despite the prostrations of both the driver and his assistant. She was an old, rather bulky woman totally dressed in black with a tattooed chin and forehead. She took charge of things by the very force of her personality, moving other items around so that her huge bag could fit. There were no seats left so, as the bus began to depart, the woman was the only person left standing. The aisles were full of bags and other belongings and there were also some half dozen people perched rather precariously on the engine cover next to the driver's seat, including his assistant. The woman pushed and prodded her goods aside and slowly, slowly, lowered herself onto the engine cover as well, somewhat displacing the people already there to the extent that one young man, who had incredibly long fingernails on both of his little fingers, almost fell into the driver's lap.

During the course of the trip, the Bedouin woman shouted amiably at the driver and she occasionally hit him as well, to sort of emphasise a particular point, none of which I was able to understand. She hadn't, of course, purchased a ticket before quitting Aleppo and started a huge argument with the driver's assistant when he tried to charge her for the trip. She ended up insisting that he give her some money. However, she subsided at last and pulled the required fare out of some secret fold in her dress.

The rest of the trip to Hama was uneventful. From time to time, the bus would stop to let some people off or to pick up people that waved the bus down from the roadside. The driver's assistant would then collect fares from these people, most of this money probably ending up in either his or the driver's pockets.

Once we arrived in Hama, we headed for the Cairo Hotel which was at the time one of the cleanest, best run and friendliest hotels in Syria, as well as being one of the cheapest. It cost 350SL ($7 US) for a room with two beds - and clean sheets, a private bathroom and a television. The owner of the hotel spoke perfect English, served us tea and chatted amiably.

Hama was the most attractive town in Syria. It hugged both sides of the Orontes River and boasted numerous norias – wooden water wheels some 20 metres in diameter that were built centuries ago to carry water up from the river into canals to irrigate nearby fields. Most of the norias still functioned, although mostly for show, and the sound of their creaking when they slowly turned as the weight of the water pushed them could be heard in many parts of the town.

Bullet holes from the 1982 massacre could still be seen on some of the buildings around the town, however it was otherwise a really peaceful place to spend a couple of days. We walked along the river and sat in a coffee house drinking coke and, eventually, Arak, watching a group of boys climbing up the norias only to dive and jump from impossible heights into the filthy, dangerous river. Later, we visited the hilltop where the remains of the old citadel were to be found and finally ended in a garden café by the river. While the cafes are 'men only', they certainly tolerate women (especially foreign women). Small groups of older men were seated at tables chatting quietly while in the background the faint groaning sound of the norias could just be discerned. We sat down, ordered tea, a nargileh (water pipe) and a backgammon board and spent the next couple of hours drinking, smoking and playing backgammon. After the initial shock of seeing a woman smoking a nargileh no one took any notice of us, except for one old man who was missing an arm. He shuffled over to us, insisting on showing us how to play backgammon. We shared our tea and our nargileh with him.

It was about the most relaxing moment of my life. The nargileh gave me a sense of euphoria, yet the clacking of dice and backgammon pieces kept the mind alert. We shared the nargileh, each taking a couple of drags in turn before turning the mouthpiece towards us and proffering it to the next person. The flattened ball of tobacco sitting on top of the main part of the nargileh slowly roasted as we smoked and from time to time one of the waiters would come and add a new piece of burning coal on top of the tobacco.

I thought back to the first time that I visited Hama, in the early days of Saddam Hussein's invasion of Kuwait which was before I ever thought I'd one day live in Syria. We had stayed at the same hotel and walked almost the exact same route along the river past the norias and up towards the citadel.

In the citadel park we met a young man who spoke a little English. He wanted an opportunity to practice so we sat on the grass and chatted with him for a while. He was Jewish and said that while many of his cousins had left Syria for Israel, his family wanted to stay. His father had a good job and they felt their life was good. They didn't feel any particular enmity from non-Jews. As far as they were concerned, they were all Syrians.

He invited us to tea in his home. Their apartment was fairly typical for Syria. Looking back on this experience once I had moved to Selemanieh, I realised that the apartment was about the same size as ours, although certainly cleaner and better furnished. There was no power when we arrived, so the interior of the apartment was quite dim as the overhang on the balcony blocked out much of the natural light. The walls were painted green. The young man's mother and three sisters were home and they looked just like any group of Syrian women in their own home, wearing either trousers or comfortable dresses.

We were served tea and as the afternoon wore on, they brought out a selection of bread, hummus, salad and kibbeh to eat. The power came back on as it began to get dark outside, which brightened the room just a little. The younger brother and then the father came home and joined us. By this stage, I remember that we had no idea how we were going to extricate ourselves as we had no idea whether leaving would cause offence or whether not leaving would cause offence.

The father then suggested we go to a concert that was being held that evening, so he and our young man host took us to a courtyard surrounded by a beautiful building with archways and ornate wooden carvings where a group of about 100 people, mostly men, sat on stools or on the ground in a semi-circle and listened to five men sing and play a variety of instruments.

My second visit to Hama was with my parents when I had managed to persuade them to spend a few days sightseeing in Syria after driving with me from Geneva. We had lunch in a park overlooking several norias before driving to the Crac des Chevaliers (a fortress used by Richard Lionheart during the Crusades) in the afternoon. That night we had driven back to Homs and had had some difficulty finding a place to stay. After trying several hotels that looked particularly sinister, we drove into the centre of Homs – quite precarious, as the streets were very narrow and at times I wondered if the Range Rover would even make it around some of the bends. Anyway, we had finally found a sort of travel agency that was open and I had asked for a hotel recommendation. The agent closed up his shop and accompanied us to a place that didn't even really look like a hotel from the outside.

There had been a 'suite' available, so we took it. The price was not much more than the Cairo Hotel in Hama, so I wasn't expecting much. There were two quite large rooms with two beds in each. After a quick dinner, my parents and I had gone to bed, however it was some time before we were able to get to sleep as there was a lot of party noise coming from the building next door. Eventually it died down.

About an hour later, the telephone rang in my room, waking me up. I picked it up and a man's voice said 'telephone, telephone'. I tried to ask what he wanted, however I couldn't make myself understood. I hung up. The phone immediately rang again. I picked it up, 'telephone, telephone', said the man. I rung off and left the phone off the hook.

A couple of minutes later, there was a banging on the door. My father and I went to the door and tried to ascertain what the issue was without actually opening the door. We couldn't make ourselves understood, so I put some more clothes on and opened the door. The man said the telephone was off the hook and needed to be put back on – at least, that is what we understood him to say. My Arabic at that stage wasn't all that great, and he didn't speak any English, so there was a lot of miming going on. I mimed that the telephone kept ringing and waking us up. However, he insisted that the phone be put back onto its hook. The man then left and we all went back to bed.

About an hour later the early morning call to prayer began and I swear to this day that all the loudspeakers were trained directly onto our rooms. All I could hear from my parent's room was a sort of hysterical laughter of my mother's, followed by dad's suggestion that we dress and leave for Damascus.

There are a couple of quirky postscripts to this story. First, when we checked out of the hotel, they charged us for the telephone calls.

The second occurred about a month later when I drove out of Syria to spend the night in Turkey and then re-enter Syria by a different border in order to either delay or hopefully prevent my car being put into the 'gentle' custody of customs (I was successful). About 10pm there was a loud banging on my hotel room door which woke me from a deep sleep. When I called through the door to ask what the issue was, a man said 'telephone telephone'. I went to pick up the receiver and found it was dead, so I informed him of this. 'Telephone telephone' he said again. I opened the door and he gestured in the direction of the room across the hall from mine; the door was ajar. I went in and picked the telephone up. It was for me! I had met an American earlier in the day and he had been trying to find me to see if I wanted to have dinner with him. He'd called several times, however the hotel manager had, at first, told him that I was out. There had been no light in my room and the possibility that that meant that I might be asleep hadn't occurred to him – it had been too early in the evening.

The experience in Homs was enough to encourage me to ensure any future travel plans did not end with an evening in Homs. Hama was a vastly superior destination. However, Homs was essentially in the centre of Syria and operated as both a terminus and a starting point for buses and service taxis heading North to Hama/Aleppo, South to Damascus, East to Palmyra and the desert and West to the coast, so I became rather familiar with the place.

The morning after my third visit to Hama, we took a service taxi to Homs. These taxis were supposed to take only five passengers, however exceptions could always be made. We got crammed into the back of the car with two women and two children, while the women's husbands sat in the front with the driver. Fortunately, it was about a 30-minute drive so our muscles didn't cramp too much.

From Homs we caught a local bus heading towards Tartous, alighting about an hour into the trip at the bottom of the hill, some 12km from the Crac des Chevaliers. I had visited this, the 'Knight's Castle', twice before and it was a wonderful example of a crusader castle. The crusaders began construction in 1170 and, once completed, it could garrison some 4000 knights. It had been well preserved and was one of Syria's primary tourist attractions. It sat majestically at the top of a hill that commanded a 360-degree view, able to easily spot any invasion force coming from any direction.

When we got off the Tartous bus, a Belgian woman joined us and asked if we knew the best way to get to the castle. There was a pickup waiting at the bus stop so I went and asked if he would take us to the castle. 'Not a problem,' was the response, and the cost would be only 100SL, each.

Problem. I told him 'no way' and walked off. The other two people with me were somewhat disconcerted. We did not want to walk 12km up the hill. However, in Syria one never needed to wait long for other opportunities to materialise and after about five minutes of walking a local bus (essentially a minivan) ambled by and we squeezed in for the price of 5SL each. This bus dropped us towards the end of the village, still five kilometres from the castle itself. We could see it standing there, majestically, just out of reach.

Not to worry. We weren't the only tourists on the local bus, and we had also been joined by this stage by several of the castle guards who chatted to us as we started walking. About two minutes later a pickup came by and we all piled onto the back. This took us a further three kilometres closer, for no payment at all. Then, an even smaller local bus came by and picked us all up. He didn't charge us either, however we all gave him 5SL and he dropped us at the castle door.

Several hours later when we left the castle, we flagged down a pickup, the owner of which very kindly drove us out of his way to where the bus comes along. He wanted no payment at all. While waiting for the bus with two locals, a taxi came by and one of the men negotiated a ride back to Homs so we joined them and had a fairly comfortable trip back to town.

Palmyra – the jewel in the crown

Palmyra is an ancient Semitic city located almost in the centre of Syria. It is probably the most famous of Syria's many treasures and has become more famous, or infamous, since 2015 when civil war hit and many of its ancient ruins were destroyed.

I visited Palmyra many times. From whatever road you drove towards the town, the mirage of Palmyra would start to glisten out of the surrounding desert and slowly transform from that mirage into reality.

Occupation of the oasis of Palmyra dates back to Neolithic settlements, where nomadic tribes began trading, and slowly turned the village into a caravanserai. Palmyra, or Tadmor, is located on what were the major trade routes that ran both north-south between the Black Sea and Yemen, and west-east between Europe and China.

At one stage of Palmyra's history, during the third century AD, the power of Palmyra was almost enough challenge the might of Rome. Certainly, its Queen, Zenobia tried through the establishment of the Palmyrene Empire. She was defeated in 273 and was reputedly carted off, in chains, to be the star attraction at a Triumph in Rome.

There were two distinct parts to Palmyra – the ancient ruins and the 'modern' town. The ruins were a bit like visiting Pompeii and the Roman Forum, all in one, with a whole lot of other bits added as well. As you arrived, you first went right through the middle of the ruins. In fact, the road did a sort of dog leg, so you ended up having the stunning archaeological remains surrounding you on both sides of the road.

To the North lay a steep hill, on top of which sat the Mamluk Castle, named Fakhr Al Din Al Ma'ani, and at the base stood a series of burial tombs. All around, beyond the ruins, one could see palm trees – from whence the town's name had come. Palmyra was built along a wadi – a depression along which water could flow – and had a permanent water source.

The first time I visited Palmyra we were backpacking and arrived in the 'modern' town by an ancient bus that had broken down some half dozen times during its route between Damascus and Palmyra. We had a travelling backgammon set and after about five minutes of waiting during the first breakdown, we got it out and set it up, just in time for the bus to start again. After the second breakdown, everyone in the bus superstitiously watched us set up the board, expecting that its completion would start the motor again. In fact, they were right – so it became a rather fun game to the satisfaction of everyone, especially the driver.

Anyway, we arrived just after lunchtime to find the cheap hotel closed for the afternoon. There was a sort of coffee shop next door. I mean, it sold coffee and a few bits of things to eat and had three or four rickety tables, however otherwise didn't really resemble much of anything. Anyway, we ordered a couple of colas and the owner suggested we leave our backpacks in the corner for the afternoon. With some trepidation we opted to do that and spent a few hours walking all over the ruins. It was a most amazing feeling. Not only were the ruins spectacular, but they were also just there. You walked along the road and straight into them, on either side. There was nobody trying to sell you tickets, or trinkets, or maps, or drinks, or food, or anything. There was no-one. We had the ruins to ourselves.

There was a long street (over one kilometre) with 10-metre-high columns on either side, an agora with much of the sides still standing, and a very well-preserved Roman theatre. (Fast forward in time, and the theatre was used for public executions in 2015.)

The Temple of Bel was just magnificent. During this, my first visit, much of it inside was in ruins. It was first built in 32 AD, after all. However, over the next few years I visited Palmyra many times and watched as archaeologists slowly put the temple back together.

It is incredibly distressing to know that this Temple has now been destroyed, along with many other masterpieces of the past.

This propensity to try to obliterate all evidence of the past is probably saddest when one considers that, in a place like Palmyra, the archaeological ruins showed a different, multicultural and largely tolerant past existing in Syria (and Iraq) that was established in antiquity and continued through the Islamic Period. Those destroying these artefacts are attempting to create a brutal monocultural reality, while at the same time harvesting much of this heritage to sell on the black market, which seems to imply contradictory ideas at play.

Anyway, back to my first visit. After wandering around the ruins and going through the little museum, we returned to the place where we had left our luggage. Nothing had been touched. We checked into the hotel next door and returned to the sort of café for a dinner of rotisserie chicken.

The second time I visited Palmyra I was with my parents. They were somewhat less keen to try the really cheap hotel so we, at first, tried a more glamorous one right next to the ruins. However, we were unable to explain what we wanted to the woman in charge, and she didn't appear to want us to stay anyway, so we ended up at the five-star hotel a little further out of town, across the road from the ruins.

This hotel was sumptuous inside. The lobby was large and domed and included a bar and a lot of very comfortable looking sofas, chairs and tables to one side. We were provided with two rooms and escorted down a long corridor to typical up-market hotel rooms.

The hotel boasted a large swimming pool and we asked if it was open, as we could see no-one around. No, the pool was closed, however it wasn't a problem, they would open it for us. While we were swimming, we were asked if we would like to visit a cave where one could swim and take a therapeutic mud bath.

This was too good an offer to pass up, so we followed one of the hotel staff across the road to an inconspicuous door that, when opened, led down a long badly lit staircase into the dark. Faint rustling noises from the ceiling proved to be a large group of bats, with the odd one or two flying around overhead.

Part way down there was a large alcove in which you could leave your towel and any clothes you had. Once you continued to the bottom of the stairs, flickering lights revealed a large cave with clean, cool water and pools of mud to one side. The cave led to a whole system of interconnected caves, although we didn't wander far as the lights didn't continue beyond the first cave. It felt a little strange, however it was rather fun to squish mud onto our bodies and then swim in the shallow clear water, while bats flew overhead and at times disappeared beyond the lights in the cave.

These caves were probably used by previous inhabitants of Palmyra, dating back beyond the Roman era. I wondered how it might have been in those times with, perhaps, slaves carrying down candles to light the water's edge.

We had one scary moment when the lights went out. The darkness was total and absolute, even though it was still daylight outside. The darkness lasted only about one minute, although it was a huge relief when the lights came back on, presumably due to a power cut and a subsequent generator kicking in.

After showers and a change of clothes, the three of us met in the bar for pre-dinner drinks. Other than three staff, there was no-one else there. In fact, the hotel was almost empty of guests.

Mom ordered a coke; I had a glass of wine and dad asked for a gin martini. The waiter taking our order went back to the bar and conferred with his two colleagues. He came back to dad to confirm his order: 'a gin martini'.

We watched as he returned to the bar and one of the men on the other side of the bar walked to the other end and brought back what looked to be a book. He flicked through some pages and then all three studiously examined what he had found.

While mom's and my drinks were being poured by one of the bar staff, the other appeared to be carefully following instructions. He had pulled down off the shelves both a Gordon's gin and a martini bottle, so it seemed like the right place to start. There was a bit of jiggling and some other movement that was hidden by the other two hovering men, and a colourless liquid was finally poured into a martini glass.

The waiter carefully carried our drinks to the table, placed them and returned to the bar, where the other two were now intently watching us. We all kind of watched as dad slowly lifted the glass to his lips. He took a sip and gave the three men a thumb's up. They all returned huge grins: they had gotten it right.

To confirm their success, dad ordered a second drink and they were clearly delighted.

Then we went into dinner. There were a couple of other people in the restaurant, however the huge dining room was mostly empty. It was the middle of the week, and I later learned that this hotel was full every weekend and was used by occasional tour groups. Otherwise, it had little patronage from passing traffic.

The menus were in both Arabic and English and offered an extensive selection of food. My parents quickly ordered in English, however I had by this stage been learning Arabic and wanted to show off, so I ordered in Arabic. The waiter looked puzzled, however he didn't say anything and headed off to the kitchen.

Some 20 minutes later he brought dishes for my parents, however nothing materialised for me so, given the dishes were enormous, we shared the two. Once back in the hotel room I looked up what I had ordered and found out that I had asked for a rapier. Perhaps the waiter thought I was deranged, so opted to take the path of least resistance and ignore me. It was a good lesson and served me right.

Hashing, or an excuse to drink

Hash House Harriers (or H3) is an international institution that originated in 1938 in Malaysia when a group of British colonial officers and expatriates began holding weekly 'paper chase' or 'hare and hounds' runs. Although affected by the Second World War, the group was formalised in 1950 with its own constitution. The objectives were:

To promote physical fitness among members;

To get rid of weekend hangovers;

To acquire a good thirst and to satisfy it in beer; and

To persuade the older members that they are not as old as they feel.

Apart from the excitement of chasing the hare and finding the trail, harriers reaching the end of the trail would partake of beer, ginger beer and cigarettes, which doesn't really sound much like the promotion of physical fitness. However, one cannot argue with success, as the idea of H3 became something of a phenomenon after 1950 and Hash House Harrier groups have formed all over the world, mostly in places that expatriates congregate.

We had an active social club attached to ICARDA, where I worked. Its facilities were near the international school and included tennis and squash courts. We also played softball and held social events in a small hall that included a bar.

Starting the Halab Hash House Harriers (H4) seemed a logical extension to this. We held the first ever H4 at the Byzantine ruins of Baquerha and Kherbet Khatib near Bab al Hawa in the hills about 40 kilometres north-west of Aleppo, with two runs looping around, partly on the gravel road, partly along sheep and goat tracks and partly just over some extremely stony ground through and around the small olive orchards and grazing areas.

I was one of the three 'hares' that went out to the site in the morning to lay the two trails, using whitish gravel to mark them. It was, at times, hard to find the trail as many of the stones on the hillsides were a similar colour. However, that was considered part of the charm of the hash. Trails were not supposed to be too easy to follow and they were meant to include lots of false trails and dead ends, so that the slower 'hounds' could keep up with the faster ones.

Some 50 people participated in the first run, including some dozen nationalities with ages ranging from under five to over 50. At the runs' conclusions, hares and hounds alike would be accused of a range of misdemeanours such as running too fast or too slowly, or not completing the second half. The punishment was to down a bottle of beer (or for the teetotallers, soft drink) and, if the drink couldn't be finished, have what was left poured over one's head.

Syrian beer rarely had a head itself, which made it something of a struggle to drink at all, let alone 'drink it down'. It was almost preferable to have it poured over you, especially when many of the later hashes took place near water bodies providing an opportunity to swim yourself clean.

Following the 'down downs', hash participants would sing and international participants meant the selection of songs became, over time, quite eclectic. We learned choruses in Sinhala, Hindi, French, Arabic and Australian as well as animated action songs from all over the world.

At the time that we started the H4, there were some restrictions on the types of group meetings or activities that could be held in Syria. It is now quite easy to see why the Syrian Government did not encourage public gatherings, as there was the risk that dissatisfaction and riots could ensue. There were certainly onlookers at every run. Syrian locals shepherding their livestock, working in the fields or orchards or simply travelling along the tracks and roads we used were frequently to be seen. They never seemed to mind us creating a bit of a ruckus, however they never asked if they could join in, either.

Anyway, the Syrian police had some concerns about the creation of the Halab H3, despite the fact that a H3 already existed in Damascus. The police insisted on coming to the second run to see what it was all about.

The second run was held at the Afrin River and comprised just one long trail instead of the two shorter ones created for the first outing (although it did have a half-way point to allow for some liquid sustenance). The countryside was quite hilly and there were practically no tracks other than the odd one carved out by dozens of sheep and goats passing that way. The home base (start and finish) was at the end of a very bumpy track culminating in a cool, refreshing stream and the trail wound up and down the hills, going through the stream several times.

Three police officers turned up in their car, two in the front and one in the back. The officer in the back seat was half sitting, half lying across the seat with his legs crossed and poking out of an open window. They asked what format the meeting would take. When told the participants were going for a run, they gestured expansively with their hands and said, 'lead on', in full expectation that they would be following us.

They changed their minds when they realised their car would never be able to follow the run. Instead, they lounged quietly under the shade of some olive trees to wait until everyone was back. They accepted some drinks, however they did not volunteer to participate in any singing nor did they swim in the stream.

I am not sure how they reported back to their superiors. It might have been that the group was considered too crazy to incite any rebellion. The Halab Hash House Harriers was there to stay. It was actually a wonderful way to visit some of the many ruins around Aleppo. Syria, having been invaded and conquered many times, contains ruins dating back over 10,000 years. It has been an archaeologist's paradise. There isn't much left of value to find, although when I was living in Syria, there was a black market for archaeological finds. The government tried to control archaeological digs, however given the extensive numbers of ruins and limited financial means, it would have been difficult. During my first year in Syria, we began excavating a mound at Tel Hadya, the research station where I worked, and found an old burial site with bones and pottery shards. The government asked us to stop further work on it, as we were not experienced and might damage something of value. No further work was done on that site while I was living there – it was fenced off – however, it is likely that whatever was there has now been destroyed.

H4 runs took place approximately once a month and many used the ruins of the dead cities of northern Syria as their backdrop. There were approximately 750 ruined sites in the general area, including some 150 churches, most dating back to between the fourth and seventh centuries. The population in the area at that time would have been greater with a thriving export-oriented economy centred on olive oil. Rainfall patterns over the centuries have demonstrated a strong cyclical nature and reduced rainfall may have contributed to population decline. The villages may also have been abandoned when trading opportunities disappeared and there was no alternative to the monoculture of olives.

One thing is certain. Syria has withstood many invasions, conquests and economic, cultural or religious revolutions in its 10,000-year history and it will certainly survive the current one.

International diplomacy

Syria achieved its independence at the end of the Second World War after nearly 30 years under French rule and some 500 years of Turkish occupation. Due both to its largely Moslem population, who understandably are not pro-Semitic, and to the fact that it wanted to get rid of its mandate rulers, Syrians generally sympathised with the Germans during World War II. As a result, there were large numbers of Allied troops stationed in Syria during both wars, not only the Free French, but also members of the British Commonwealth States, including Australia and New Zealand.

Foreign troop war cemeteries have been maintained in Syria, with graves dating back to both world wars. In Aleppo, there were two war cemeteries, one for German troops and one for the Allied troops. While the Turks were enemies during the First World War, they were allies for the Second and their dead were buried in a corner of the Allies' cemetery rather than in the German troops' cemetery.

On the closest Friday to November 11 each year a special ceremony was held at the Allies' cemetery in Aleppo with Ambassadors from several nations in attendance. The Allies' cemetery was a little out of town, nestled inside a small park with trees and grass and a cenotaph in the middle. It was peaceful and quiet although very sad considering how young and how far away from home those that were buried there were when they died. They came from many countries, including Belgium, France, England, Australia and India.

The ceremony comprised short speeches and the laying of wreaths, followed by a lunch reception. At the reception, I met one of the Allied Ambassadors who happened to be quite youthful given his position, and unmarried. He told me that he was in Aleppo not only for the Remembrance Day ceremony, but also because he was escorting a 'fact finding' tour of a group of politicians from his country. They had been invited to a cocktail reception at the home of a colleague of mine from ICARDA and he asked me to accompany him.

I felt a little like a gate crasher, however fortunately the Ambassador had warned our hosts that I would also be in attendance. It was a pleasant evening and rather amusing to be flirted with by an ambassador. He told me that he was planning to go to Wanas for dinner following the cocktail party and would I like to accompany him?

The evening was still relatively young when the group said its goodbyes to the hosts. A minibus provided transport for the group of politicians, however the Ambassador had his own limousine, complete with the country's flags moving in the slight breeze on the vehicle's bonnet. The chauffeur opened the back door and the Ambassador ushered me inside.

As the chauffeur climbed behind the wheel, the other front door opened and one of the embassy staff members started to get in as well. She took one look at me sitting on the back seat, and asked 'would you prefer me to travel in the bus?'

'Yes, please,' was the reply and we were left to ourselves, other than the chauffeur in the front.

For a tiny, brief moment, I confess I gave a small thought to the future. Could I possibly see myself as 'Mrs Ambassador?' We chatted all the way to the restaurant and while he ordered food and drinks. It did seem almost like a fairy tale – an ambassador was about the closest to a prince that I would ever get, after all – and he was attractive, funny and a great conversationalist.

However, about halfway through the meal I changed my mind. Mr Ambassador spilled a drink all over the table and on one of our dishes and, by the meal's conclusion, had also consumed most of a bottle of Arak, at least that which he hadn't spilled, in addition to whatever he had been drinking since lunchtime and at the cocktail party.

I finally couldn't stand it anymore as all meaningful conversation had ceased and Mr Ambassador was slurring his words. I suggested we leave. He literally staggered out of the restaurant and piled into the car. The chauffeur asked me where I lived and I gave him directions.

In the backseat, I now found Mr Ambassador had given up on diplomatic niceties. He tried kissing me and began pawing in the general direction of the front of my body. Fortunately, he was still a diplomat at heart (or he was too inebriated) so didn't pursue matters when I quite forcefully pushed him back to his side of the vehicle.

The streets by this time were almost completely empty and the buildings dark and quiet. The only light came from the odd streetlight. Everyone in Selemaniah was fast asleep, for which I was partly grateful but mostly disappointed! Here I was, being driven home in a beautiful limousine with flags, and there was no-one to witness it.

When we arrived at the corner of my street, I told the chauffeur to stop. He leaped out to open the back door for me and asked where I lived. I pointed to the building, looking somewhat dingier and more crumbly than usual, and said I'd be fine from here. I think the Ambassador had fallen asleep. I'll never forget the expression on the chauffeur's face; it was a quirky sort of bemusement that I think came from a whole jumble of thoughts, although mostly that the Ambassador had just chauffeured someone to a building and an area of the city that was definitely not of a class that the Ambassador would normally associate with.

I never did see the Ambassador again and have often wondered if he would even have had a memory of the dinner when he awoke, with what I expect would have been a massive headache, the next day.

Happy birthday, Jesus

For Christmas I went to Deir Ezzor to join Basel's family. Basel was in Australia. Most of his family lived in Syria's eastern-most town, which straddles the Euphrates River and is famous for a bridge the French built during the days of colonial rule. The population was largely made up of Bedouin who had settled in town and most of the industry was geared towards servicing the rural population – nomadic Bedouin herders and farmers cultivating irrigated crops. In the late 1980s the town also boomed thanks to the discovery of oil in the desert nearby. Several foreign companies had offices in Deir Ezzor, although they tended, for example Shell, to keep most of their foreign staff in Damascus.

There were some one hundred Christian families living in Deir Ezzor, a tiny minority in a population of over 100,000 people. Together they managed to maintain three churches: Greek Orthodox, Armenian and Roman Catholic.

I joined Basel's mother, Oom Akram, at Basel's brother, Akram, and sister-in-law, Hala's, place. Christmas preparations began on December 24 with a huge house cleaning effort. A man was hired to wash down all the walls and floors and all the furniture was scrubbed. Cooking also went on all day. I had asked to attend a midnight mass – something I normally did at Christmas – and Hala said she would go with me. However, as she was fasting – it was a tradition amongst the Orthodox to fast on Christmas Eve – dinner wasn't served until 11.00 in the evening. I had dressed in a suit and she was wearing a glittery dress she had made for Christmas and at the meal's end we left. I drove her husband's car as she didn't drive.

However, there had been something of a misunderstanding. Hala informed me that she had to pass by the hairdresser's first and this gave me an opportunity to glimpse this most important event in the women's social calendar: the night before a major celebration. It also meant that I missed midnight mass, as I didn't realise how long a trip to the hairdressers could take. The salon wasn't only a place where one went to have one's hair done: it was essentially the female equivalent of the coffee houses frequented by the men.

We pushed open the door and entered the smoke-filled room, shutting out the dark, frosty night behind us. Cries of exclamation and delight emanated from the women already present. Hala indicated a chair to me by the door and passed across the room to kiss her kinswomen, crying out her relationships to each one to me as she did so. I nodded and smiled shyly to each one as I heard, through the haze of conversation, my position in society situated with complete frankness. 'Ajinabieh (foreigner), a friend of the brother of my husband. But ajinabieh, you know,' she said. The women nodded and stared and asked more questions. What was I doing here? How did I come to be here? Did I speak their language? Further questions escaped my ears as I sat in the corner.

I knew that, as a woman, one should never look sloppy when leaving the house. In the privacy of one's own home, it was OK to lounge about in a faded dressing gown and scuffed slippers and even to welcome visitors in such fashion. But in the eyes of the outside society, as a woman dress was all-important, as was the make-up and hair style. Although my suit was reasonably well-cut, I was no match for the other women dressed in bright glittery contraptions studded with articles of gold. Cleopatra-like eyes – heavy with kohl on both the upper and lower lids – were uniform and their hair, well that would come. It was for this reason that they were here, in this room, close to midnight on the same night that, nearly 2000 years before, a certain baby had been born in a stable not that many hundreds of kilometres away.

Babies were certainly a central subject of the women's conversation, but not that one in particular, who had given them all a reason to be meeting here. Christmas was a high point in their annual social calendar and hair styles required perfection.

'Did you hear that my uncle's sister's son's wife is pregnant again? So soon after her last. She hopes this one will be a boy.'

'My cousin's uncle's wife just lost theirs. So sad, but really she is too old for another child.'

'Too old, she's only 40. My cousin's mother had a baby when she was about 42.'

'How many months are you now pregnant?'

'Four.'

The conversation continued. Chattering and laughing across the room, with one of the women having her hair pulled and piled twisting herself around to contribute. The man performing the task dragged her back around, ignoring the conversation. He backcombed her hair, sprayed it, smoothed it down again and began curling the bottom, dragged the whole lot up again and began pinning it at impossible angles on the top of her head.

One of the women waiting for her turn disappeared into the back of the salon, only to emerge some five minutes later with half a dozen cups of coffee – the usual tiny cups that held only a couple of mouthfuls of coffee, but which contained more caffeine than a normal, Western-style cup of coffee. There were more than six women present, so the first couple refused politely, having quickly calculated how many cups needed to remain on the tray in order to allow everyone the chance of accepting a cup.

The contortions that the hairdresser put himself into were fascinating to watch, as he seemed to wrap his arms in tangles while deftly maintaining brush, comb and several pins between his teeth. The results were the most elaborate styles I had seen to date, with well-polished masses protruding at all sorts of angles. I couldn't help but wonder if all these women were planning to sleep sitting up that night, or whether they would bother to go to bed at all.

Hala asked for her hair to be pulled tightly back from her face, and then carefully massed into the shape of a 1940s-style box hat, sitting jauntily, slightly right of centre. The following day she would attach a dangling ornament from it, almost like a tiara. While it sounds weird, it seemed to fit her personality and her dress.

Of course, by the time Hala had finished having her hair done it was after one in the morning, so church was out. We went home again to find the family still awake and chatting quietly and shortly afterwards we all retired to bed.

It seemed that only five minutes passed of actual sleep time before we all had to get up again and begin preparations for the day. Hala's two children, twin girls aged about two years old, required washing and changing, which she achieved only with the constant screaming and screeching of the infants who did not want a bath. To counteract the cold weather, Hala dressed the two girls in layer upon layer of clothing so that they looked like two little round balls, topped off with matching red frocks, followed by cream woollen capes and hats. In fact, I wore only a suit and no coat, as although it was winter it was not all that cold. However, Syrian women loved to dress their children warmly.

After the mandatory photo session, we headed off to the Greek Orthodox Church where the service was well underway. The men entered the church towards the front while we women, accompanied by the children, went into the back. The church was crowded and we only found seats as some other women were in the process of leaving. In the front half of the church I saw row upon row of men, all sitting straight, silent, solemn. In contrast, around me were squirming children and giggling women, who whispered excitedly to each other while the Priests droned their prayers.

At the completion of the service all the men rose and filed around the front of the church, crossing themselves in front of various icons and before the altar. They helped themselves to pieces of bread and left offerings of the monetary kind in a waiting golden dish. We followed on behind, a more undisciplined group, the women holding their children up towards each icon so that the children could brush their lips across them. The women, too, often kissed the statues and photographs.

Once outside the church we milled about the enclosed courtyard while the sun, almost completely overhead, beamed down unseasonal warmth onto us. A multitude of handshakes and kisses and 'Merry Christmas' were exchanged and I was passed from one stranger to another, managing to forget all their names one second after they were announced.

From church we began a series of home visits where the pattern was the same. On entry we were ushered to the best lounge in the house, where the seats may well have been freshly cleaned or had had their customary plastic covers removed. Small glasses of a very sweet wine - not unlike sherry - would be served, followed by plates of candy and sweets, of which we had to take at least one of each type. After some 20 minutes of conversation, we would rise and wish each other Merry Christmas once more, before leaving just as another group arrived. We would then move on to the next house.

We eventually made it home and sat down to a late lunch, most of which had been prepared the day before. The table groaned with the feast, comprising tiny cigar-like rolls of vine leaves stuffed with rice and spices and swimming in garlic; several different types of kibbeh, which is cracked wheat pounded with minced lamb and filled with a lamb mixture and either baked, boiled or fried; roast lamb, stuffed eggplants, an array of vegetables and hummus and other dips, bread and rice. There were several different kinds of dessert and we washed it all down with red wine from Layla's village, Mahardeh, which was reputed to make the best wine in Syria.

Following the lengthy luncheon, we very quickly cleared up, for we had another function to attend: a children's Christmas party at the local five-star hotel. Akram tossed the car keys to me while I mentally tried to calculate how many glasses of sherry and wine I had consumed since Church. It didn't bear thinking about and for once I was pleased that Syria didn't have any drink driving laws. The car had no car seats for the children, of course, so Hala had to try and control the two squirming toddlers herself. I drove very slowly.

The function turned out to be in a sort of conference centre next to the hotel: quite an impressive place, with uniformed ushers to guide us into the muddle of women and children. I think every Christian family in Deir Ezzor that had children were present, along with many that did not have children as well. Long tables were arranged throughout the room, each one piled with food. In one corner scratched a band and some of the older children were dancing.

Our two quickly fell asleep, one of them nestling her head into my shoulder which restricted my movement somewhat. I had thought that the band might play some Christmas carols, but it seemed to prefer the more regular Arab repertoire. However, my wish was finally granted. As Santa Claus arrived, complete with a huge sack filled to the brim with plastic toys, the band launched into its Christmas song, and sang it in English to an English tune: 'Happy birthday to you, happy birthday to you, happy birthday dear Jesus, happy birthday to you.'

When it came time to leave, I found that I was expected to drive four other women and their respective children home, bringing the count of total bodies in the car – fortunately a station wagon – up to 14. The women chatted and gossiped, the children screamed and kicked, and I almost tore my hair out as directions on where to go came from five different mouths and 10 gesticulating hands. Finally, I managed to drive the wrong way down a one-way street straight towards a policeman, who blew his whistle and rushed over to my window. As I rolled it down, he gazed with incredulity at the foreign woman driving a car overloaded with women and children and he could do nothing but wave us on.

After finally arriving home we all managed a couple of hours sleep before the commencement of yet another Christmas function: a Christmas dance, back at the Conference Centre. The children's toys and balloons had been cleared and fresh plates of food placed on all the tables. The lights had been dimmed and beer and arak flowed, rather than the soft drinks of the afternoon. The band continued to scratch out its music, but for the evening omitted its Christmas song and no Santa appeared.

I found myself in a large party of cousins and relatives of Basel and, while most of the men were married, they all accompanied me on the dance floor at least once. The form of dancing fluctuated between the more usual pair dancing one finds anywhere in the world – although Arabic style (a sort of gyration of the hips while waving your hands more or less over your head) – and line dancing, which I had learned while attending a Bedouin wedding. This consisted of holding the hands of people on either side of you and moving slowly around in a counter clockwise direction, copying fairly intricate foot movements so that the whole line dipped and rose in unison and moved to the right at the same time. It was fun but quite energetic and after some 10 minutes faces would perspire and the grip of hands weaken with accumulated sweat.

Once during the course of the evening an eligible gentleman from a nearby table approached our own and asked Akram if he could have a dance with me. He had obviously spent some time sorting out relationships at the table and had concluded that Akram was the male most closely related to me.

Forbidden contacts

Syria was essentially a Moslem country, but like any other place in the world, sex was a preoccupation for many people. One's image of a Moslem country is of women veiling their sexuality, a phenomenon which countries such as Saudi Arabia have taken to extremes, where one sees nothing other than men and black sacks walking the streets. Perhaps the total lack of feminine presence heightens the awareness of the opposite sex, or perhaps the fact that sex, except of course between two married people – married to each other, that is – is essentially forbidden, makes it so very appealing.

At any rate conversations, particularly with Syrian men, often turned to sex. To begin with, I thought it was simply because I was a foreigner and in the eyes of a Syrian man that meant freedom in the most liberal way, sexually. In short, many men thought that sex with a foreign woman was as inevitable as that the sun would rise. I was at a luncheon party one day shortly before I was due to leave Syria for a few months and got into a conversation with a Christian Syrian who I had met only once before. He had been invited by a girlfriend of mine, with whom he was going out. Suddenly he leaned across and whispered in my ear, 'you will find the time to make love with me before you go, won't you.' I wasn't sure if my shock was due to the question, the way it was put, or the fact that he was supposed to be my girlfriend's date! Shortly afterwards he got up to leave and asked if I was free that night.

'Nope,' (I said).

'Tomorrow?'

'Nope.'

'Sunday?'

'Nope.'

'Monday?'

'Nope.'

'Next Thursday?'

'Nope.'

'Guess I'm out of luck, then.'

'Yep!' I didn't see him again.

Wearing a wedding ring didn't always help, either. The guidebooks suggested a wedding ring, as it would add an element of respect in a Syrian's eyes. For the most part this was true and I adopted this strategy during most of my time in Syria, although it was awkward not being able to produce a husband at will and several different men took on this role when visiting from overseas. This made things more complicated still, as I had to keep track of what name my 'husband' went by for different people. But one incident always stands out in my mind as the classic example of the image some Syrian men had of European women.

It was my second day in Syria as a tourist, well before I harboured any thoughts of ever living in the country. I had travelled to the Middle East on holiday with my boyfriend and of course we posed as a married couple. I had also gone out of my way to look as unattractive as possible: old, baggy clothes, long sleeves and trousers, hair tied back and no make-up. In the Omayyad Mosque in Damascus, we met a young engineer who invited us to his brother's place for lunch.

There were several other men at the house, including a stocky, balding man aged about thirty-five who taught Arabic language and literature at the university. He spoke quite good English and we got into a conversation about teaching methods, as I had been teaching English as a foreign language to put myself through university in Europe. After about half an hour, we were asked if we wanted to wash before lunch, so the teacher took us down the stairs (the lounge was on the first floor) to the bathroom, which was the traditional kind with just a large knee-level sink from which you dipped a bowl before pouring the water over the bits of your body you wished to wash.

My 'husband' washed first, the teacher pouring water over his feet and hands. The teacher then suggested he return upstairs. He immediately began helping me to wash, insisting on rubbing the soap into my feet himself, and suddenly he launched himself onto me, trying to kiss me. I beat a hasty retreat and started back upstairs.

'You have not finished washing,' he implored, running after me.

'I have quite finished,' I replied haughtily, and returned to the lounge to sit on the only sofa. My 'husband' and our host were engrossed in a game of backgammon on the floor and there were no other people in the room. The teacher returned shortly, his hair wet and I presumed he had taken a shower to cool his ardour. I was wrong – about the ardour bit, I mean – as he immediately came and sat down beside me. I moved. He moved. I moved, he moved and put his hand on my knee, moving up the inside of my leg, all this with my 'husband' sitting (his back to us) just two metres away! The game finished just then so I moved again and made frantic signals for my 'husband' to come and sit between us and fortunately he understood.

The remainder of the visit remains burned on my memory. It was a painful meal, with the teacher trying to favour me with the tastiest morsels of food which I was, for politeness, forced to swallow after they had been totally pawed by him. The atmosphere grew very tense, as his eyes bored into me, trying to consume me where I sat. All we were really doing was trying to work out how to extricate ourselves without causing offence, because everyone else in the room was really nice. We did finally leave, the teacher and one other accompanying us on our route, and so began a St. Vitus dance so I did not have to walk in close proximity to him while, of course, his objective exactly opposed my own. When we finally parted ways, he kissed my 'husband' twice and then a third time. I could see his mind calculating that he may get as many from me. He came to claim them, but I stepped away and distantly put out my hand to shake his. Without a word, he turned his heel and stalked off. I should conclude by saying that the other young man was upset at his friend's behaviour and apologised about it, commenting that I was the first European woman he had ever had contact with, which was why he had acted so strangely.

I experienced another interesting incident that showed there were some rather warped ideas about western women. One cool and clear evening, Mahmoud and I walked from Layla's and my apartment in Selemanieh to a party that was actually being held in the courtyard house I stayed in during my first month in Syria. It was dark and the road we were walking along was curiously empty of both traffic and pedestrians, other than one lone man we saw walking towards us.

As he reached us, he murmured something to Mahmoud, who responded very angrily. The man walked on. It turned out that he had asked Mahmoud how much I cost.

Another incident that still has me occasionally shaking at the thought of how easily it could have ended in, well, much more than tears, also took place in Damascus. ICARDA ran a car service, normally daily, between Aleppo and Damascus ferrying staff, family and goods. There were two guest houses that we could use in Damascus, one reserved for the higher echelons (although we could use it if a room was free) and another, where the drivers also stayed.

On this particular day, there was only the driver and me. I was picking up a girlfriend who was flying in from Europe and we were going to stay one night at the second guesthouse. Anyway, the driver and I had a good chat during the four hours it took us to get to Damascus and by the time we arrived at the guesthouse it felt like we were old friends. He turned the television on in the lounge and I made some tea and sat on the sofa with a book. I felt it wouldn't be very companionable to take my tea and book and sit in the bedroom on my own.

The driver took his tea and headed off to the bathroom. About 10 minutes later I saw him out of the corner of my eye standing in the doorway with just a towel wrapped around his waist. He seemed to be hesitating, as if to work out which direction to head. Of course, at the time this didn't really register consciously with me. However, as I can still picture every moment of those agonising seconds, I well remember his hesitant movements.

Having come to his internal decision, he moved extremely fast and before I knew what was happening, he had launched himself next to me on the sofa, went to fling his arms around me and said, 'kiss me'.

Thankfully, my amygdala kicked in extremely quickly and I jumped as far as I could away from him, dropping my book and folding my arms across my body while shouting 'NO' loudly enough for people in Aleppo to hear. It is funny, as I can sort of see the expression I had on my face, which must have scared the guy so much that he immediately backed off.

I never reported him. I carefully considered my conduct and realised that I had been rather friendly with him on the drive down. I had so much enjoyed the fact that he made an effort to understand my strange Arabic, and he had perhaps over read my friendliness. Anyway, I was lucky as he didn't press himself onto me as I guess it could have ended badly.

How do the women feel?

SYRIA, ALTHOUGH ESSENTIALLY a Moslem state, had a secular government so there were no laws concerning the dress code. In fact, it was one of the country's beauties, the richness and variety of dress that could be found. On a street in Damascus or Aleppo, you could simultaneously see a man in a business suit, another in jalabiya and scarf and a third dressed casually, while the women would range from being totally covered - face included - in black to mini-skirts. Women in black abayas were Moslem and those with head scarves usually were as well, although older Christian women also frequently dressed in black and sometimes wore scarves. Girls of all religious backgrounds would dress smartly with elaborate hair styles and fashion jewellery. For the most part it depended on the family, as some women were forced to cover up, either by their husbands or fathers. Some opted to do so themselves.

While beautiful women could be seen in Syria and some of the fashion could be considered daring for a Moslem country, there was a large enough difference to Europe or Lebanon for anyone, men and women included, to gape with amazement at scantily clad women after even just a little time in the country. This in turn heightened people's awareness of sex and could give some of the totally covered women, particularly when they moved well, a heavy aura of sexuality and a desire for others to see what lies beneath the coverings.

As I've already described what can lie underneath the black abayas (at the wedding), it is normal for men to wish to experience such sights as well. Moslem men would learn once they married. Prior to their marriage, most Moslem men had little opportunity to indulge in any form of intimacy with the opposite sex. Nor would they normally socialise with women, as the social lives of men and women were generally segregated. But what about the Christian men? Their women were not veiled and there was plenty of social contact, so their imagination might not necessarily have run quite as wild as those of their Moslem brothers. Would they ever have the chance to learn what there was behind the veil?

Apparently, some of them did. The heightened awareness of sex was not only a man's prerogative; it was a woman's as well and, in many ways, even more so. Women were taught from an early age that they must veil themselves because it is they who are the devils who drive men wild. They were told men had no control, so must ensure that no man was ever aroused by seeing any part of their bodies. Then they were sometimes forced into arranged marriages with men they didn't even like. It was normal for them to want to find out what all the fuss was really about. However, sleeping with a Moslem man was not really a viable option, as he could talk and the woman's reputation could be, at the least, shattered. She could even be killed. So, such women would turn to Christian men, who were considered safer prey.

One of my friends, a raggedly handsome Armenian, told me he had often been propositioned by Moslem women. I was witness to such a conversation one evening as we sat in his shop. A girl came in asking to use the telephone and through this intermediary, she arranged a rendezvous with a man at a place nearby. Then she sat down. Conversation between us had ceased, waiting until her departure, and Nurses, my friend, had picked up a newspaper and I a book I had been holding. Silence reigned for two minutes, before the girl said, suddenly,

'Marhaba'.

We both looked at her, but she was addressing Nurses only. As they were speaking in Arabic, she must have thought I didn't understand, as we had been talking in English when she walked in. I pretended to ignore her and concentrated on my book.

'Why don't you speak to me?'

'Why should I? You have used the telephone. Can I help you in any other way?'

'What is your name?'

'Nurses.'

'Are you Moslem?'

'No, actually I'm Armenian,' an obvious fact from his name which was pasted over the counter. The name ended in -ian, which denotes an Armenian. And Armenians are Christians.

'What are you doing today?'

'I'm working.'

'Do you often go to Kassab?' Kassab was a resort on the Mediterranean Coast, popular with Christians.

'Sometimes.'

'Maybe next time you go you could take me with you.'

'Inshallah.' (If God wills).

'I have just returned from Canada. Do you know Canada?'

'No.'

'What about the States? I went to New York. I hated New York. They are terrible there.'

'I liked New York.'

'I kept thinking someone would rape me.'

'Why would anyone want to rape you? I had no trouble.'

'Were you alone?'

'No, I was with a friend.'

'Male or female?'

'Male.'

'You should have gone to San Francisco. It is better for men there.'

'I am not interested in men.'

'They would find you very attractive. But women would find you more attractive.'

Nurses did not reply. The conversation had taken a totally pointless direction and I was mortified. She couldn't see that he was not at all interested in talking to her, yet she continued on, blindly. Finally, she picked herself up, announcing that she was going now, and no-one stopped her. So, she left.

It took some time to recover from that visit, but after a certain amount of laughter at the girl's expense Nurses sobered up and told me that this sort of thing happened many times, and not only with fashionable girls. Propositions had also come from girls veiled in black 'sacks'.

'One day I decide to go with one, you know, to see what it is like, how she think,' Nurses said. 'This girl come into my shop. She come in many times, always covered in black, just her face open. She say 'can we meet? What you do for lunch?' I say I went home or to a restaurant. She say 'can we meet?' I say, 'OK, sure we can meet; we can go to a restaurant.' She say no, she want to go somewhere where we can be private, you know? I ask her if she want food. She say anything, but she must meet me somewhere. She cannot walk in the street with me and well, I don't want to either. I cannot walk by a Moslem girl dressed in black. So I buy a chicken and we meet some place. We arrive and, well, I am hungry. She say no time for food, she has only one hour before she is missed, and she start to take off her coat. I say 'wait a minute, we must talk.' No, she say, no time to talk. But I cannot do it like this. I tell her we must talk, but she not interested. She only want me. After she ask me for some present or money but I say no and she don't expect it really.'

The Swiss Watches

In general, Syrian men seemed much more concerned with sex and romance than women. Many Syrian women admitted to me that they had never been in love. They married for security and to have a home and children and they didn't really expect love and romance. If it came, they considered it would last for only a brief period between the date of the engagement and the date of the wedding. After marriage, reality would hit home.

Marika, a friend of mine, told me once in front of her husband that she had not loved him when they got married. 'That is true, isn't it?' she asked him, but said that she fell in love with him afterwards. However, one evening she quite candidly stated that she knew he visited prostitutes when he was out of town and she accused her brother-in-law, in front of their mother-in-law, of doing the same thing.

Syrian men dreamt of romance, however they had little idea of how to be romantic. Basel never bought me flowers or whispered sweet nothings or treated me in any of the ways deemed traditional amongst lovers, yet he frequently described himself as being 'too romantic'. They did believe in love at first sight and they set up images of perfect harmony in their minds. Unfortunately, the way Syrian society was constructed meant images were doomed to crack, because in reality men and women led totally separate lives. Women would nearly always calculate the man's worth before accepting him and a man knew that he must amass enough to be able to provide a home and certain other amenities prior to being able to get married. Therefore, marriage unions tended to turn into contractual arrangements.

I think this preoccupation with romance, to say nothing of sex, was one of the reasons why Syrian men sometimes gravitated towards foreign women. In fact, there were two types of men who chased after foreign women: those wanting what they considered to be easy sex and those looking for romance.

I used to catch the bus to work with another foreign student, Ann, when I was still living in Shahaba. One day, as she mounted the bus, I could tell that yet another crisis had occurred in a strange, twisted affair in which she had managed to become involved. She rolled her eyes heavenwards as she saw me and turned to flop down in the neighbouring seat.

'What's happened this time?' I asked, ignoring the usual niceties of 'hello, how are you?' It was obvious how she was: stressed out and confused.

'Oh, you wouldn't believe what's happened now,' she said, shaking her curly hair, still damp from a rushed shower, and flinging her face into her hands. 'I just can't believe it myself.'

'So you saw him last night? You told him it was over?'

'Yes, but no. No, I couldn't. You know, I ended up bargaining for my free time. Actually bargaining - bartering - you know, like I was an item from the market. He refused to stop seeing me: he said I was the only thing that had happened to him to give him a reason to go on living and that I had to accept seeing him.'

'So how often are you to see him now?'

'I said I would see him once a month, not more. He said no, once a week. We then bargained and bargained until we arrived at once every two and a half weeks - exactly every two and a half weeks, not a day more and not a day less. It's more than I can bear!

'But can you imagine,' she said, turning tired hazel eyes towards me, 'actually having to bargain for my time? I must be mad.'

We were talking about Ann's 'affair' with a strange man who had chosen to fall in love with her over the purchase of a potted plant. Weeks earlier Ann had joined me in the bus after a hectic weekend during which she had bought the plant and been escorted to dinner. This may sound fairly mundane, however such occurrences could become high spots in an interesting, if somewhat quiet, existence in Syria. The man, Abdullah, owned the plant shop and was, by all accounts, part of the city's 'elite' society of merchants and businessmen, mostly made rich through wheeling and dealing on the black and grey markets. Immediately taken with Ann, Abdullah invited her to the most luxurious eatery the city boasted, the rooftop restaurant in the five-star hotel, the Shahba Sham, where an imported French chef provided gastronomical delights at outrageous prices, to be washed down with genuine French wine. Ann accepted on the condition that they be accompanied by at least one other person, so Abdullah brought along his 11-year-old daughter. Ann told me it had been a pleasant evening, although Abdullah talked non-stop and was rather boring company. His life story had emerged, including full details concerning his wife's sudden death ten months earlier and his own lapse into depression following this event.

Two days later Abdullah invited her to a local tennis match in which the country's cream players were performing. This was followed by an appearance at a basketball game. However, by this time Ann had been put off Abdullah: he had talked non-stop throughout both events and more than once during the tennis match neighbouring spectators had had to verbally request that he be quiet. This had mortified Ann and she said, when relating these incidents to me, 'it isn't as if he even says anything worth saying. He just talks for the sake of hearing his own voice: he's so boring.'

So I suggested she stop seeing him. At least he was being a gentleman and had not even attempted to hold her hand at any time or request a kiss. Ann agreed and, over a coffee the following afternoon, informed him that she would not accept another date.

Abdullah was devastated. 'You can't do this to me,' he whined. 'I think you are wonderful, and you mean so much to me now. You are helping me to get over my wife's death.'

However, Ann remained adamant and they parted, each in a foul mood. At work the next day Abdullah's sister, who worked at ICARDA, went to see Ann.

'Please', she begged, gazing at Ann with sorrowful eyes as she sat across from her, leaning forward in order to physically enunciate each word. 'Please continue going out with my brother. It's the first time since his wife died that we've seen him happy. He's fallen madly in love with you and does nothing but talk about you at home. You must keep seeing him. Help him and help us to find himself again.'

So, Ann accepted and that evening Abdullah, his greasy black hair swished back and stuck down over his crown, his designer clothes tucked neatly over his bulging stomach, bounded eagerly into Ann's apartment, his eyes alight with joy. In one hand he carried a large bunch of pink and red carnations and in the other a jewellery box containing an expensive Swiss watch. After presenting these and refusing any argument that he take at least the watch back, he handed over a third gift, an invitation to a local fashion show which was something that could not be had for any price outside the elite inner circle of high flyer socialites.

Ann, dressed in her usual baggy jeans and loose T-shirt ('what's a skirt?' she once asked me when summoned to a formal dinner party at work) suddenly realized that Abdullah was a ticket to a social life which no foreigner could ever normally aspire to, but at what price? Was it really worth the price, a chance to glimpse this upper-crust lifestyle?

Two dates later she had decided. Yes, it was interesting – no, fascinating – to experience the crème-de-la-crème at their intrigues and games. Nameless faces at the 'elite' swimming pool at the Shahaba Sham, to which foreigners were admitted because of the dollars they represented, suddenly became acquaintances. Abdullah even bought her a season ticket to the pool. However, the price, Abdullah's constant and boring remarks, was too much to pay. Once again Ann tried to end the relationship and now, apparently, she was to see him every two and a half weeks.

Next to me Ann sighed as the bus wound its way up the hill to our offices. I looked at her, the gold watch shining in the early morning sunlight and catching my attention, as she turned and twisted her hands in agitated movements.

'And I'll have to face his sister this morning. He's sure to have told her and I'll get an earful. I think I'll go and hide in the lab, where she can't find me.'

Over the next two weeks she said little about Abdullah. However, as the two-and-a-half week break neared completion I noticed a certain uneasiness overtake her spirits. We were both invited to a special function the evening of the termination of the two-and-a-half-week period, however Ann declined the invitation.

'Why aren't you coming?' I asked. 'You could ask Abdullah to change the day, can't you?'

'No, he'll refuse to wait one day extra before seeing me.'

'Well, see him on Thursday instead of Friday, then,' I suggested.

'No way! I'm not seeing him one second earlier than what we agreed to.'

I passed a very pleasant evening Friday which seemed more than what Ann had experienced when I saw her the following day. We joined a walking group for a day's excursion in a range of hills a few hours' drive from home.

'Ugh, it was horrible', she said. 'Abdullah took his daughter and me over to the coast for a swim and on the way over we had an accident. He was, of course, showing off, driving far too fast and we hit a pickup coming the other way. We were so lucky not to end up at the bottom of the cliff. He's so stupid. I can't see him again, I just can't. I can't go through with all this.'

She strode out angrily and I had to jog to keep up with her as we climbed a hill sprinkled with olive trees. She berated herself as she marched along.

'I must be mad. Why can't I just tell him to go to hell? How did I get myself into this?' She picked up a rock and flung it at a tree, causing a loud thump and crack as a piece of bark split and tumbled to the ground along with the rock.

By the end of the day Ann was laughing again and with darkness we arrived at my place and proceeded to create something edible for dinner. Suddenly Ann grasped her wrist and cried.

'Hell, I've lost my watch!'

'Where? How?'

'It must have fallen off during our walk. Hell. I'm going to have to tell him.'

'No, you don't.'

'Yes, I will, he'll ask me for sure where it is if I'm not wearing it.'

A week passed. Small lines of strain formed around Ann's eyes as she contemplated the scene with Abdullah when next she saw him. Then she received an invitation from his sister to dinner at her house for two days' time. Not knowing what to do, she accepted. When the day arrived, Ann went to ask the sister, Noor, where she lived.

'Oh, it's OK', Noor said. 'Abdullah will come and pick you up.'

Furious, Ann rounded on Noor. 'This is not part of our bargain. Abdullah and I agreed to see each other every two and a half weeks. I didn't want to see him at all, but you asked me to continue to see him. I refuse to allow him to break the agreement like this. I'm not coming tonight.'

Noor was upset. 'You must come. We are all expecting you to come. The whole family is looking forward to this evening.'

'Well, I'm sorry, but it is not part of the bargain. Abdullah knows that.'

Later in the day, an apologetic Abdullah telephoned Ann, begging her not to be annoyed but he would respect the agreement. They would not see each other for another week. That evening a large flower arrangement arrived by courier to Ann's house.

On 'D' date day, Abdullah took Ann out to dinner again. The following morning Ann groaned her way onto the bus.

'Did you tell him about the watch?'

'Yep. He noticed first thing that I didn't have it and he said he would buy me another. I told him not to, but I guess he probably will.'

'How was dinner?'

'Oh, OK. There was another couple there, friends of his, so I spoke to them all night. However, he does like to show off. When he paid the bill, he brought out a huge wad of notes and counted all the money in front of me, as if to prove that he was spending lots of money on me. He can't hold his alcohol, either. He only had a couple of beers and got very red and silly. I had to drive him home.'

With the weight of guilt about the watch lifted from her mind, Ann returned to her usual bouncy, amusing and slightly hair-brained self. Ann sometimes acted exactly according to the image of an absent-minded mad scientist. She dropped test tubes, lost lab notes, spilled chemicals and claimed to be utterly disorganised. Out in the field she never wore a hat so during the harvest season her perky nose reddened and peeled, while the freckle population across her cheeks would propagate. One morning she claimed to have left her bag at home and announced to the world in general that she was a silly dozy ass. It was only on arrival at work that she realized her bag had been sitting on her lap the whole time. It was good to see her return to just being dozy and creasing me up with tales of chemical disasters and green-eyed monsters.

One day, well before the two-and-a-half-week period was up, a subdued Ann boarded the bus in a pensive mood. This was most unusual for that hour of the morning, particularly as she usually just managed to race under the shower, throw some clothes on and grab an apple for breakfast before the bus appeared. In fact, she was usually still asleep, at least in mind, as the bus lurched away. I asked what she was thinking of.

'Abdullah telephoned me last night.'

'That's not part of the agreement,' I observed.

'No, but he wants me, as a favour, to see him tonight. It is the anniversary of his wife's death and he doesn't want to spend the evening either alone, or in the company of his family which will just depress him more.'

So, she went and spent the evening holding his hand while he blubbered on her shoulder. He also presented her with another watch, an exact replica of the first one. In addition, he began talking of a future together. He wanted to marry Ann. She reminded him so much of his wife, he said. Not her looks, but her mannerisms, her bouncy cheerful ways. Ann would make him so happy.

'It is now sure,' Ann told me. 'I have to stop this. I can't keep seeing him, it isn't fair on him. Each time he sees me he falls more and more for me and as for my reminding him of his wife! I have to tell him it is finished for good.'

So she did and Abdullah took it, although quite badly. In the ensuing weeks Ann received, every Thursday afternoon, a new bouquet of flowers. The accompanying cards never gave a name, but only said, in Arabic, 'be happy' or 'God be with you'. Finally, after a month of regular flower deliveries, Ann told the man bringing the flowers to return them to the sender and that she would refuse any more.

'But Abdullah's a good man', the courier insisted. 'Why do you refuse to see him?'

Ann refused. Unhappy, the man left and the flower deliveries ceased.

This should be the end of the story, but there is one final twist to it. Ann was fated to have all Abdullah's gifts to her wither away like their relationship did. The flowers, of course, all died. Even the potted plant, the item which began the whole affair, collapsed after a week without water and refused to be coaxed back into health. The T-shirt he bought on the coast had chemicals spilled all over it, creating large holes. And finally, the same day – Ann must have been more dozy than usual that day – her second wristwatch did not survive a full cycle in the washing machine. (Don't ask how it came to be washed.) When it emerged parts had turned green and water sloshed over the face. Its ticking days were definitely over.

Bluebells in May

The month of May arrived and the weather cleared. Rain stopped and the daily temperatures soared. In fact, that month turned out to be incredibly hot and we baked inside the apartment. Even at night, I would lie naked on top of my bed in the draft of the open window, yet in the morning the sheets could be wrung out.

In compensation, clothes took at the most one hour to dry. On the downside, the apartment suddenly got terribly dusty again, after a fairly dust-free winter. An hour after dusting, a film would gather on the furniture again and even daily dusting would not keep the apartment clean. In addition, for a few weeks we waged war on cockroaches. These creatures seemed to invade even the cleanest of homes, and ours was not the cleanest. I found myself killing several a day. This was a relatively easy task as an extremely effective spray was manufactured locally that killed them on the spot. I wondered how many Layla was killing, as we rarely saw each other at this time and never mentioned cockroaches when we did.

One evening she came home to find me hopping about the kitchen, spray can in hand, while two large black beasts eluded my efforts by hiding in cracks under the rim of the sink.

'I hate cockroaches,' I cried in greeting, landing spray on their scurrying backs before almost prancing in gloating triumph as they died. Layla was torn between looks of disgust at the cockroaches and bursting into laughter at me.

'How many do you kill each day,' I asked, raking them up into the garbage.

'None,' she replied. I gaped in amazement.

'I don't kill any because there doesn't seem to be any point. It's just that there are so many of them,' she explained in a small voice, a little piteously.

'But Layla, if you don't kill them, they grow into bigger ones and then have children. If you kill them, you kill potential productivity. We have to kill them to get rid of them.'

She hadn't seen it that way and a couple of days later I found her lining up targets with the spray can with relish. With our combined efforts, in a week the cockroaches had gone.

From the first of May, women in blue dresses began dotting the streets of Selemanieh, like bluebells. The dresses were all sky-blue and mostly terminated at the wrists and below the knee. Around each waist was hung a white rope belt. At least half the women walking around Selemanieh would be dressed in this fashion, with only slight differences to the theme, as some women chose white dresses and blue belts, and some girls wore sky-blue blouses with jeans, topped off with the white rope belt.

The women wore these clothes for the whole month of May. Then suddenly, on the first of June, they all changed back again into their normal clothes. Only one or two lingered, like late maturing bluebells hanging on to life after the rest have perished. By mid-June all the sky-blue dresses were gone, put away until the following year.

What was the significance of these blue dresses? I longed to ask each woman as she passed me in the street. Instead, my imagination bounded through numerous reasons. Of course, I knew the basic intention. Sky-blue was Mary's colour – the virgin Mary, of course – and May is her month. Christian women would promise to wear the sky-blue dresses for the whole month in return for some little act of God, such as a pregnancy, passing exams, health, a husband, or countless other reasons and it was easy to see how one's imagination could burst with ideas at the sight of each woman. There were, of course, others who wore the blue dresses because it was part of their religious culture and perhaps not everyone had a wish to be fulfilled.

Syria's two Easters took place at the beginning of April and the beginning of May. At the beginning of April, I did the traditional round of the churches with Basel and Nabil. It was Good Friday and woeful wailings from all the churches filled the streets of the Christian quarters, almost drowning out the Mosques at the lunch time prayer. Most people walking the streets were dressed in black and to complete the scene, the weather was cold, windy and rainy. Black clouds raced across the sky, throwing heavy shadows on the already darkened ground and the air was gloomy. We walked up to one of the Orthodox churches, gathering with crowds of other people to witness the march of Jesus. As it was late afternoon, he had, symbolically, already died on the cross. He lay, a life-size statue from the front of the church, across a pall with a light gauze covering his body. A bell moaned, a Christian youth band marched to a mournful tune, incense was waved about and the body of Jesus was carried through the crowd, around the square and back into the church. This action was repeated several times before people began moving off, either towards other churches or inside the church to receive benediction there.

We chose to visit some other churches and witnessed similar processions in the Latin Church and the Armenian Church, where we received our benediction. This was in the form of a piece of cotton wool dipped in oil. Basel and Nabil both pressed their lips to the cotton wool and made the sign of the cross in the air with it.

On Sunday morning I decided to go to church. As there were no Protestant churches that I knew of, I presumed that the Roman Catholic Church would provide the closest service to that which I was used to. The church had a series of continuous services from seven in the morning until one in the afternoon and I joined the throng for the 11a.m. service.

The church was packed full. I knew no-one there so sat, rather self-consciously, at one end of a pew. I watched the people as they arrived and amused myself with trying to guess which colour was most prominent. Finally, I decided on blue, but the profusion of colours and hair styles had turned the church into something mildly resembling a fashion parade. Then the singing began and the priests, accompanied by swinging incense and the cross, paraded up the aisle.

There were no hymn books or service books and everyone, at the right moments, murmured the prayers and sang the hymns from memory. Yet I found to my amazement that I could follow the service almost word for word, despite the different language (the service was in Arabic, of course) and different Christian sect. The order of service and the prayers were practically identical to those we used to have 'at home'. However, my amazement quickly turned to sorrow as I thought of 'home' and my family. It was the first time in months that I had felt really homesick. To rid my mind of such thoughts I concentrated more on the sermon than I ever had in the past and managed to understand its general gist.

A month later, the Orthodox Christians celebrated their Easter. I went to Layla's village for this event, only to discover that people in Mahardeh did everything differently to anyone else. While I accepted that they didn't celebrate Easter with most of the world - they were, after all, mostly Orthodox at Mahardeh - I learned that they didn't celebrate Easter on the Sunday, like the other Orthodox do, either. Monday was their important day. They argued that the bible categorically states that Jesus rose three days after his crucifixion, and Sunday is only the second day. So, on the Orthodox Easter Sunday, I found myself bar-b-queuing four different sorts of meat and fish in a sunny spot overlooking a Crusader Castle, the Orontes River and the Ghab Valley, where a huge government project had developed irrigated agriculture so well that it had become a stunning picture of small, interconnecting fields in a rainbow of greens and yellows and browns.

On Easter Day, the Monday, we dressed for church. As the event was to be the usual 'souk al-banat' (female market) fashion parade, Layla and I decided to go all out and get our hair done. The salons in town were all doing a roaring trade on a semi-production line basis, but we found one that had time for us and we were quoted a price of 100 pounds ($2 US) each. There were two stylists, a youngish man with a well-trimmed beard and a middle-aged woman, whose uncombed and dirty hair I hoped had not yet been touched that day. She was also dressed in an old smock and wore nothing but men's work socks on her feet.

While we were waiting, watching the amazing hairstyles being created on other customers, a large, rather ugly girl entered the salon. Her hair looked as if something had been done to it: it was thick and shiny and fluffed up, but she was obviously not happy with it. She sat down next to me, almost immediately getting up again to admire herself in the mirror. She turned this way and that, checking all angles and she then sat down again and leaned over me to reach for some nail polish. It was a bright purple and she applied it liberally over her nails.

Then it was my turn. I got a brief shampoo and they then began operations with the drier and spray. Another woman entered the salon and spoke to the fat, unattractive girl with purple nail polish, telling her that she had to 'come home'. I immediately guessed a mother-daughter relationship. The daughter then said her hair needed fixing, as she looked awful. 'No, you don't, you look beautiful,' the mother lied, kindly, but the girl burst into tears, large watery ones, which reddened and blotched her already acne-covered face. Everyone immediately rallied around her, which only made her sob all the more. It was finally agreed to redo her hair and the girl stopped crying. The final result did not improve matters much, however she seemed to feel better about it. I felt sorry for her, because she must have felt that in the Mahardeh cattle market of women, she was the runt.

When both Layla and I had been fluffed and dried and sprayed, we were charged 100 pounds for the two of us. They refused any more, saying that it was a special offer for us, because we were first time customers.

In anticipation of the day I had, earlier in the week, purchased a new outfit, comprising a calf-length skirt and fancy, matching waistcoat, accompanied with a mildly frilly blouse which didn't look too out of place alongside the totally 'over the top' creations that many of the other girls were wearing. Layla was similarly dressed to me, although she had opted for fashionable wide-bottomed trousers instead of a skirt.

Her family had already left for church by the time we were ready to go so we walked together up the street, passing large groups of people standing chatting by the roadside. Many other people joined our march up the slight incline to where the large Orthodox Church stood, commanding one of the highest points in the town. It was a large church with a wrought-iron fence surrounding a large courtyard, with the church sitting gracefully in the centre. Stone steps running the full width of the church front led up to several doors that admitted entrance to the church itself, and once inside one had the choice of sitting in the main area of the church or mounting yet more stairs to huge balconies that spanned out along either side of the building. We opted for the latter route and I shortly found myself pushing through a fairly thick crowd of people to the edge of the balcony. Some 20 metres across from me I could see a similar crowd pushing in their turn and, looking down, I was awarded with a wonderful view of near silent chaos, as people, their chatting voices kept to a low drone, moved with frenzy through the aisles. There were a lot of people sitting as well, however it seemed as if almost as many were taking seats as were leaving, perhaps because they suddenly caught sight of someone they knew, several pews forward (or behind). More and yet more people arrived and the costumes and colour were spectacular. Most interestingly, for me, was that most of the older members of the congregation - and there were many of them - were not dressed in a lavish, modern style at all. Rather, they dressed as the Bedouin do in the steppe and desert in black robes with scarves wound around the heads of the women, and jalabiyas with mostly white scarves on the men. I was used to seeing such dress in my working life, as I spent so much time with the Bedouin, and I found it hard to separate the Bedouin I knew with the elderly people sitting in the church here. Given the Bedouin were all Moslem, I found it difficult to marry the dress and the Christian religion together.

The elderly people and their 'Bedouin' dress merely served as harmonising units, islands of tranquillity, in the chaotic mass of colours, not unlike a plain, dull stitch in an intricately patterned jumper, or a strip of darkening blue in a vivid sunset. For the most part the elderly remained calm, seated, waiting for God and for the most part they were dressed in dull colours; black, black and grey, with black or white scarves covering their heads. Some opted for the more brightly coloured scarves with splashes of red, blue or orange, however they were mostly uniform, men and women alike.

Out of one corner of my eye I suddenly saw a slightly more organised movement congregating at the church entrance and moving slowly, like an incoming tide, up the aisle. It was a procession, passing almost directly beneath me. The low murmur of chatter did not cease, not did the movement of people into or out of the church, but the procession, taking no heed, made its way purposefully towards the altar. Leading the file was a robed man carrying a cross, followed by other robed men, all dressed in white with cream crosses embroidered on their backs. One of the company carried aloft a beautifully bound bible and the people sitting or standing to either side of the parade reached out for the book to touch and to then kiss their fingers in reverence.

The Priest, I presume he was, finally reached the altar, but the movement and chatter still did not cease. I had never felt less in a church. In a loud voice, to carry his words above all other noise, he calmly announced that as Basel, Hafez Al-Assad the President's son, had been killed earlier that year, Easter was cancelled, and we should all be in mourning.

Shortly after this announcement everyone, it seemed, rose as one and all tried to leave the church at the same time. People pushed and shoved to be the first out of the doors, only to stop immediately on exiting and commence chattering with a neighbour, effectively blocking the door for any followers. I half held onto Layla's shoulder as we wound our way back down the stairs again, totally bemused, trying to work out what was actually going on. Easter cancelled?

Once outside, some 20 crowded and sweating minutes later, Layla explained the event a little more clearly. Easter in Mahardeh was normally accompanied by parades and music and laughter and fun. That was the main part that was cancelled, in memory of Basel. However, that still did not explain the lack of a service, and I wondered how we going to justify all the new clothes and hairdos.

This question only had time to enter my mind before it was answered. Layla's uncles and some cousins found us and, together, we began promenading up and down the road. We were joined by some new people and others left us behind as we stopped to gossip with other groups along our route. At one stage we entered a doorway and climbed a short flight of stairs to a parlour teeming with people, Layla's parents included. Each person held a coffee cup and saucer in their laps. Sweets were forced on us before we managed to beat a retreat.

After an hour of walking up to the end of one road and back down another before repeating the scene, we turned into a cafe and ordered some cold drinks. No sooner had we done so, when we were joined by yet another cousin and a friend of his, that I recognised from an earlier visit to Mahardeh.

His name was Issam and he was a rather attractive bachelor aged around 30. Fairly short and neatly built, he had the russet-coloured hair quite common in Mahardeh and the rose-coloured skin to match, that went redder when he spoke or was spoken to. He also had the inevitable moustache and an excellent taste in clothes. Today he was dressed in a light grey suit and a bright shirt and tie that seemed to harmonise well with both the suit and his colouring. Obviously somewhat shy, he went even redder than usual on catching my eye and sat down abruptly, hardly managing to say hello.

During a previous visit to Mahardeh, Layla and I had gone out for an evening with three men: a cousin, an unmarried uncle and Issam. The men had taken us to a large restaurant with a resident band where we had eaten, drank arak and danced until about four in the morning. By this stage of my life in Syria I had become reasonably adept at Arabic dancing and Issam had obviously been rather taken with me. He danced with me all night. Towards the end of the evening, he asked if I would like to go for a ride on his motor scooter with him through the Ghab Valley on the following day. Having never visited the valley, I gladly accepted.

However, at the appointed hour the following day, Issam never showed up. I waited quite a respectable length of time before giving up and visiting relatives of Layla's instead. Late the following evening, Issam turned up at Layla's parents' house with the uncle and cousin but said no word of apology to me. He had had the grace to look rather embarrassed on seeing me and when we prepared for bed Layla explained the reason for his non-appearance that morning. Apparently, a lot of people had seen him dancing with 'a stranger' the previous evening and had immediately deduced that he had become engaged. He had not wanted to 'confirm' the rumours by being seen with me the following day.

All these rumours no longer seemed to worry him too much as the uncle, while we sipped our drinks, began teasing him for having stood me up. In defiance of this he immediately asked me if I wanted to go 'for a spin' there and then.

As a woman, one did not side astride motor scooters or motorbikes. My skirt was certainly wide enough to allow me to do so, however I was strictly instructed not to. I wasn't sure if this rule was to prevent the couple's bodies from having too much contact, or to preserve certain parts of the unmarried woman's anatomy intact. I found sitting side saddle a slippery experience and extremely hard on the leg muscles as they had to remain almost permanently taut to keep me balanced. Issam revved the motor to its maximum velocity as we took off, a full 30 kilometres an hour, and we flew down the street, only to do a U-turn and chug our way back up again towards the church.

For the next hour he took me all around Mahardeh, calmly defying gossip by shouting and waving to everyone he knew, which meant that he shouted and waved at everyone we saw. We passed some houses four or five times: by the fourth trip the residents, sitting on their lawns, no longer jumped up to wave. We passed the church three times, its courtyard now eerily deserted and the gates shut.

When he finally dropped me off at Layla's parents' house, my legs almost collapsed in protest and my arm felt sore, too, from alternatively having to hold onto the back of the scooter and modestly keep my skirt from blowing up into my face. My other hand had been safe, nestled as it had been between Issam's elbow and his ribs.

I left Mahardeh late that evening, having to get back to work, and Issam kindly offered to drive me to the bus depot. Of course, this meant that he would see me off with his motor scooter, so I had to climb back onto it, my legs still complaining, and this time precariously balance two bags as well. His attitude had certainly changed from my earlier visit, as he quite openly waited for the arrival of the bus, oversaw the loading of my bags and helped me climb aboard. I never found out if any new rumours developed following that Easter.

The Armenian Club

The garden was full. Groups of women of all ages, perching uncertainly on chairs missing backs, sides or seat boards, crowded around shaky tables. Overhead, a latticework of tree branches swayed in the warm and dying breeze, throwing shadows of filtered green across the stony ground. Harried waiters skipped from table to table, tearing off portions from used bills for the customers to use to write their orders. Bottles of cola and orange were whisked open and straws ceremoniously flicked out of shirt pockets to float in the bubbly liquid. Plates of hummus and mish mashes of aubergines and peppers were dumped onto the tables, which rocked and dipped with the redistribution of weight.

Many of the younger women there were exceptionally beautiful, with long, thick, dark hair waved or teased, spreading down their backs and flowing around moon-like faces filled with large dark eyes. Earrings joggled and golden necklaces, rings and bracelets shone in the moonlight. It was evening and the moon and stars were out. One could catch glimpses of them through the canopy of trees, trees whose trunks anchored them to the floor of the garden in a scattered melee with the rickety tables and chairs.

At every table a melange of languages could be heard: Arabic, Armenian, Turkish, French and even a smattering of English. Everyone in the garden was a foreigner, yet it was not a garden of tourists. Everyone chattering in the garden, drinking their colas and dipping torn off pieces of bread into hummus, held Syrian passports, yet all were foreign. No-one belonged.

The garden was part of an Armenian Club, a quiet, peaceful haven in the centre of bustling downtown Aleppo. Inside, Armenian Christians could shake off the confines of an Islamic society and hide from the masked and gowned traditional Aleppian women. The club was a place of sport – boys were playing basketball and tennis –

but more importantly it was a meeting place, a social focal point, a chance to laugh over the day's or the week's events.

Most of the people sitting at the tables were women, although there was a smattering of older men, and most of the women were young and unmarried. They giggled together and dashed to other tables, kissing their occupants, chattering and swapping chairs. As the evening drew on the clientele changed. By 9p.m. the younger girls and older women had begun to leave, their places filled by incoming groups of young men, home after a day's work which generally finished after 8p.m. Most had taken the time to return home to shower and change and they looked clean and smart with well-coiffured hair, their eyes scanning the girls remaining in the club. They joined groups of girls they knew and animatedly laughed and talked in their fashion, eyes continuously searching other tables, as if seeking out that special girl, or a long-lost friend.

In the background an artist sang mournfully in Armenian. The sound reverberated around the club, unconsciously touching the hearts of everyone there. Inside the soulful music lay the agonies of loss of homeland, of the chaining inside a society not its own. Here, within the confines of the club, it was possible to forget the outside world, but the song served to remind everyone there of where they were, and that when they left the club, the reality of life in an Arabic country would hit them once again.

Outside, cars and buses still honked and skittled their way around littered streets full of veiled women and staring men. Loud music still blared at every street corner and local street vendors cried out their wares and prices. Yet inside all was still. The only sound that could be heard, other than laughter and animated chatting, was the sad, quiet voice of the singer.

Many of the Armenians in Aleppo lived in Selemanieh or in Midan, a slightly lower-class suburb where most of the city's mechanics operated. They arrived in Syria towards the beginning of the century, fleeing massacres in Turkey. Although part of Syrian society, they tended to remain slightly to one side of both the Moslems and the Christian Arabs. Religious differences explained the distance from the former group and language differences from the latter. This was because many Armenians, particularly the older ones, had never bothered to learn Arabic, despite having lived all their lives in an Arab country. There were Armenian schools, Armenian companies in which to work and Armenian newspapers. In addition, as many Armenians knew Turkish, they could watch Turkish television (which was possible in Aleppo) for entertainment. Finally, there were the Armenian clubs, where Armenians could mix and mingle with complete disregard for the outside world.

However, sitting in one of the clubs one evening with three Armenian friends, it seemed to me that the singer with his mournful song captured perfectly the almost overwhelming melancholy that seemed to pervade over much of the Armenian society. It always seemed to me that the Armenians in Syria were all looking for a better life and spent much of their energy trying to immigrate to the United States, to Australia, to Sweden, to Canada, anywhere, in fact, that was away from the Middle East. While they would talk of returning to Armenia, no-one really wanted to. They would not admit that life was better in Syria though, as it questioned their desire to live elsewhere. It just seemed so sad to see a whole society rootless in Syria yet unwilling to return to their homeland and unable to settle and be happy in their present one. The singer cried of pain and suffering, with so much of it self-inflicted.

These images were of the larger Armenian society. That evening in the club, the three girls I was with were taking great care to keep their makeup intact and their best profiles facing the door. They helped each other out, pointing out when some hair was out of place, or some lipstick had rubbed onto front teeth. They laughed and chatted, yet so much of it seemed forced as if society expected them to show happiness.

The most incongruous part of the whole evening was the transformation after 9p.m., when the men began to arrive. It seemed to me that this was the whole point of the evening, the social gathering of young people, yet as the men began to arrive the women started to leave. We did as well, so I never managed to meet any men at the Armenian club.

Doctors and hospitals

My first hospital visit in Syria was in Hassakeh, a large town north of the Euphrates River, where I spent a couple of days undertaking field research. My colleague wanted to visit a friend of his who was a doctor at the hospital.

The hospital was a large, imposing building like hospitals often are, several stories high and locked well back behind several metres of high fence. The gates were kept mostly shut and were manned by guards with rifles. However, that did not prevent a crowd of people from pushing against both the guards and the gates in their attempts to gain entry. Just inside the gate, an old man lay semi-comatose on a bed, apparently bleeding, although not badly. No-one seemed to take any notice of him, anyway.

At the sight of us the crowd was silenced and parted like the red sea. The guards, after a quick word with us as to our business, let us in through the gate and as we passed through the crowd behind resumed its noise and pushing.

We walked through the front door and entered a dimly lit corridor where people staggered up and down, clutching at the walls. Doors opening off the corridor revealed patients lying on badly made beds in a multitude of sheet colours and styles. The whole atmosphere was generally dirty and sad. One or two male nurses in grey-white trousers and tops passed us by without taking any notice and we had to enter a doctor's surgery where a patient was being treated in order to extract any information as to where we could go to find our friend. To reach him, we climbed a large staircase to the upper floor, passing several groups of patients and friends. Near the top of the stairs was an open door leading to a toilet – the hole in the floor variety – which, at a glance, did not appear to have been cleaned out for a long time. Even my colleague was saddened at this sight and he mumbled something about wishing that I had remained in the car, so as not to have seen this seedier side of Syrian life. The main problem, he said, was that this was a government-run public hospital for people with no money. The private hospitals were much better.

There was, in fact, a private hospital near Basel's house, situated on a busy intersection near the unmarked border between Christian and Moslem suburbs. I arrived at Basel's house one evening to find him sitting and shaking, and apparently chain-smoking by the look of the number of cigarettes in the ashtray and the smoke in the room. His mother, oblivious to his distress, was clattering in the kitchen preparing supper. Normally a reserved person anyway, Basel had obviously not told his mother about whatever was troubling him. He did not enlighten me then either, but eventually stubbed out the cigarette and carried it to the kitchen, only to return with some plates swimming in hummus, freshly chopped cucumber, peppers and tomatoes and pickled aubergines. I asked what was wrong, but he just shook his head, glanced meaningly towards the kitchen and changed the subject by asking me to set out the supper table.

The meal was not eaten in silence, for Oom Akram more than made up for any lack of conversation on her son's part. Her latest gossip titbits were punctuated with the word 'killi', accompanied by movements of food in my direction. Killi means 'eat' and certainly there were no great inroads being made into the food, as Basel merely picked at his piece of bread. Very shortly after I had drunk the mandatory cups of tea following the meal I elected to go home and Basel accompanied me.

'I saw a terrible thing tonight,' he began, on my insistence that he tell me what was wrong. 'I had gone out to buy some hummus and was just on my way home when I passed the -—hospital. A taxi stopped outside the hospital and a woman got out carrying a little girl in a blanket. The little girl was crying, and then I saw another woman get out of the taxi carrying the little girl's legs.'

I stopped in horror. 'What?' I felt sick.

'Yes. Three women standing near me immediately fell down on the ground. I mean, they fainted. The two women carrying the little girl and her legs went into the hospital. But do you know the worst thing of all?' He stopped walking again and looked me in the eyes. 'The worst thing was that the hospital would not accept them. They came out of the hospital again and had to go someplace else.'

The hospital did not accept any emergency cases. Very few hospitals in Syria did, in fact, particularly if the patients had no money.

This seemed an anomaly in many respects, because the Syrian doctors were well-trained and operated modern, sophisticated machinery. Doctors were all specialised: there were no GPs, so that you had to have some idea what was wrong before selecting a doctor to visit. Many Syrian doctors completed their training overseas, either in Europe (mainly England, France, Germany or Russia) or the United States. Many of the European expatriates living in Syria opted to have their children in Syria rather than fly home: pre-natal care was excellent and you could have the same scans and check-ups for a fraction of the cost in Europe.

However, despite modern technology the system remained Syrian. Once I had to go for a blood test and I found myself in a laboratory crowded with people of all ages and with all manner of illnesses. Left and right, people were being given bottles and the direction of the bathrooms in which to fill them. Unselfconsciously but still with considerable dignity, they would return with their bottles and hand them over to the medical staff in full view of everyone else. It was a regular bunfight for me to get to the counter with my document announcing the tests required, as women dressed tightly in abayas, a minimum of their faces showing, shoved against yelling men in order to claim the attention of one of the two harassed male receptionists. When I finally managed to make it to the counter, having pushed and wiggled in my turn, the man gave me hardly a glance, simply circling the papers – that were written in Latin, not Arabic – asked for some money and sent me back to the waiting area.

When my name was called, I was beckoned over to a doorway leading into a small cubicle. The back wall of the cubicle was made of glass and I could see the laboratory technicians working on different samples of blood and urine. A little boy was sitting on the only chair in the cubicle while a female nurse tied an elastic band around his upper arm and thrust a needle into the protruding vein. The little boy, aged no more than five, didn't even flinch. As she slapped on a bandage the boy hopped down and, grabbing his mother's waiting hand, pushed past me back into the waiting room. As I took his place on the chair, I commented on how brave he was, eliciting a smiled reply from the nurse as she selected a brand-new syringe and needle from the pile of unopened packages next to her. Through the door I could see some 30 pairs of eyes watching the proceedings intently – would the colour of my blood be the same as theirs – while in the background I could hear many more people still fighting their way to the reception desk.

In order to visit another doctor once, I had to step over several groups of women and children huddled on the ground both inside the building and on the steps just outside. This building housed some dozen doctors, several of them paediatricians, and it appeared that the waiting lists were endless on that particular day. I had only a throat infection, however as I had been unable to make a telephoned appointment, I had to go personally to see if the doctor was free. He was not, so I had to return later in the day.

The crowd of women and children had not thinned. In fact, it seemed that the numbers had only swelled and I recognised a couple of groups from my first visit, nearly five hours earlier. Many of the children were fitful and crying, others were asleep from exhaustion, lying sprawled with only a thin blanket between them and the ground. Some were being cradled by their mothers, who seemed too preoccupied to gossip much with their neighbours except, perhaps, to swap symptoms. Eventually, I guessed, they would be seen by a doctor, but I could hardly imagine waiting here all day with a sick child or children. It was still early spring, so the weather was pleasant, being neither too cold nor too hot. As I stepped over a tiny baby mouthing a teat in its sleep, a nurse/receptionist called out a name from behind me and a group of two women and three children groaned to their feet in reply.

My own consultation was fairly quick and the pharmacist's chit he supplied me with was written in a curious mixture of English or Latin and Arabic that looked the same as a prescription anywhere in the world, in other words totally illegible. Despite this, the pharmacist managed to supply me with two lots of Syrian-made drugs, charging me less than one dollar for the two.

The other major trip to the doctor for me was to an eye specialist. My eyes had been itching and sore for about a week and one morning I woke up to find them looking all wrinkly and red. At first, I thought that I had gone old overnight, as the lids of my eyes looked like those of an elderly person. Layla accompanied me to a specialist she had heard of.

The entry to the doctor's office was through a combination of alleyways and steps that passed, firstly, clothing and shoe shops, followed by locked warehouses. There was a tiny staircase surrounding a disused lift shaft with solicitors' offices and surgeries leading off from it. On the third floor we found the entrance to the eye doctor.

The waiting room was empty of people except for a receptionist sitting in a bored fashion behind a much-used wooden desk. She was young, not more than 22, and wore a bright yellow suit with ornate red and gold sequins and buttons down the front. The skirt was long, reaching almost to her ankles, and the jacket had a high collar and long sleeves. On her head she wore a sheer chiffon scarf that required continual readjustments to keep it in place over her well-sprayed hair. Around three sides of the large room ran upright chairs so that, if full, the room could seat some 40 people. The walls were decorated with enticing diagrams of the insides of your eye. In addition, there was the mandatory photograph of the Syrian President and one of the courtyard in Mecca.

The doctor spoke no English or French as he had done his specialist training in Italy. Although I could communicate with him in Arabic, his explanation of the sickness of my eyes was beyond my comprehension and he quickly employed Layla as interpreter. However, she was unable to translate what exactly was wrong. He did assure me that he was able to cure me and, yes, the ridges and lines would disappear. The only drawback was that I would have to return each day for three days; I could not go to work during this time as I had to rest my eyes; and it would cost a lot of money.

'How much?' asked Layla.

'Three thousand pounds,' the doctor replied. By Syrian standards, this was a lot of money, about US$ 60, but we were talking about my eyes. I said to Layla that I would pay it.

'No, it is too much,' she told me, knowing that we could converse easily in English as the doctor could not understand. Detecting our hesitancy, the doctor suggested we go away and think about it. But they were my eyes. 'I'll tell him it is too much and get the price down,' she told me, and turned back to the doctor to begin negotiations.

I listened in horror and surprise as the two of them began quibbling about how much I was to pay for the restoration of my health. However, they eventually agreed on 1500 pounds, which Layla reckoned was still far too much. Three days later, after the mandatory three visits for eye washes, creams and lotions, my eyes were back to normal. To this day I still don't know what was wrong with them, however whatever the doctor did certainly worked.

The final touch was the doctor that I visited shortly before I was due to leave Syria. I had forgotten to pay the receptionist for my visit before going into his surgery, which is what usually happened. This time the receptionist had been on the telephone when I arrived and had waved me straight through as no-one else was waiting. When I emerged some 15 minutes later, I asked her how much I owed. Three hundred pounds, she indicated with her fingers. I handed her a 500-pound note and she disappeared into the doctor's office to look for some change.

Two minutes later she returned and handed me back my 500 pounds. 'A farewell present,' she said.

Moslem encounters

Most of the Christians in Selemanieh were scathing of Moslems. They accepted them into the suburb as meat, fruit and vegetable traders, but refused to socialise with them at all. In fact, Christians considered it beneath their dignity to sell meat and vegetables, so many of the shopkeepers in Selemanieh were Moslem. In turn, they enjoyed working in the Christian suburb because Christians, in general, did not like to bargain; making it easier to sell goods at the price you wanted to.

Religious differences were not a major concern at ICARDA. People that would not, under normal circumstances, become friends did so through the intimacy of work. I shared my office with a Moslem who took both his work and his family life very seriously. From a work point of view, I could not have had a better person with whom to share an office, as he was a man of few words and did not sit around socialising all day like some Syrians did. In addition, he was a font of knowledge that I dipped into frequently. However, occasionally something would eat at him and, with a suddenness that always surprised me, he would push his chair back from his computer or his desk and say, 'Enough is enough. I have to talk.'

At this point he would often bound out of his chair and pace back and forth, with considerable difficulty as the office was very small, and let off steam on whatever was bothering him. Eventually he would calm down and, half sitting on his desk or in the comfortable chair we had in the corner by the window, he would begin a conversation on some other matter. Frequently this would turn to religion. He had a very honest and open regard for Islam and followed its dictates to the letter. He neither smoked nor drank alcohol; he prayed and had a great reverence for the Koran. Through him I learned to appreciate Islam as a religion, as he often explained passages of the Koran to me in simple and clear terms. He had four children and a wife he adored, who was as educated as he and who worked in a professional capacity. She did not cover her head because, as was pointed out to me during one of our talks, the Koran does not actually stipulate that you must do so. It simply requires you to dress modestly.

My office co-worker meant a great deal to me, although I only fully realised this when, at the end of my three years in Syria, I had to say goodbye.

On the day I had said goodbye to him, Layla and I went out for a quick meal and I told her about my emotionally-charged day. As usual, we were speaking in Arabic and it sometimes took a bit of imagination to work out what I was saying. Fortunately, Layla had had 15 months of practice.

'When I said goodbye today,' I said, 'I had rain falling from my eyes.' I couldn't remember the word for crying or for tears.

In the office next door were two Christians and a Moslem and the five of us took morning coffee together each day. We were often joined by other people, Christians and Moslems alike, and I used to sit with my cup of bitter Turkish coffee and wonder at the seeming hypocrisy at work in front of me, as Christians claiming to hate all Moslems shook their hands and poured coffee out for them. If I ever questioned this, the reply was, 'Oh well, he's not really THAT Moslem, you know.'

The women working at ICARDA were the same. All departments had mixtures of Moslem and Christian women and in general they socialised together at work. Dissent only occurred if one of the Moslem women began dating a European, as unmarried Europeans, generally being Christian, were considered the prerogative of the Christians. Young, unmarried or unattached European men tended not to remain so for long, as the Syrian women saw them as being a ticket to a better and richer life in Europe. If, however, the men ended up with a Moslem woman, gossip and bitchiness abounded in the offices and the poor girl's reputation was scarred forever. The worst blow, in the Christians' minds, was that if marriage actually took place, the European was forced to convert to Islam.

No Moslem woman could marry a non-Moslem, while Moslem men could marry women from other religions. Christian women who married Syrian Moslems did not need to convert to Islam and could continue to practice Christianity. There have been many marriages of Europeans to Syrian Moslems, and in all cases involving a European man, the man first converted to Islam through a simple ceremony declaring faith in front of an Imam at a Mosque.

So, for the most part, there was communal inter-religious harmony at work. However, this harmony did not generally extend outside the office gates.

As a foreigner, I tended to fluctuate between different cultures and religions. Layla was also different in that, although from a Christian village, she had been brought up in a town primarily inhabited by Moslems. Most of her school friends had been Moslem and many of these friendships extended into her university days. Although now living in Selemanieh with mostly Christian friends, there were a couple of Moslem girls that visited our apartment on occasion who were living in digs at the university. One even fell in love with one of our close neighbours, another student, and they dated for a while. However, the girl finally told her mother, as she wanted to begin preparing her family for the possibility that she marry a Christian. Her parents immediately packed her bags, took her from the university and removed her to her own village and she was prohibited from seeing our Christian friend again.

In my circle of friends were several Moslems that were frequent visitors to our apartment as I enjoyed having dinner parties. Three in particular, who came from Morocco and the Sudan, wanted to join us one Sunday evening for the weekly Christian fashion parade in the streets. One had only recently arrived in Syria from Morocco, in fact, and was still adjusting to the cultural differences between the two countries. Although they were both Arab and Moslem countries, he admitted he was having great difficulties in Syria.

One Sunday evening we invited the three men over for a light meal, followed by a walk and dessert in one of the restaurants. I had given Mustapha, our newest friend, a map to our apartment as he had not been there before. He still hadn't turned up when dinner was ready, so we ate without him and afterwards set out for our walk.

As we clattered down the stairs past the open apartment doors through which we could see our neighbours sitting and taking careful note of who we were with, I remarked, 'I hope Mustapha doesn't arrive after we have left.'

Layla hit me hard, on the arm. 'Shh,' she said, fiercely, 'Don't mention that name so loudly.'

'Why ever not?'

'It's a Moslem name,' she whispered. 'I don't want the neighbours to learn we have had Moslem visitors.'

In fact, we found Mustapha standing forlornly on our street corner, holding my map upside down while trying to work out which street was which. It didn't help that few of the streets had names at all and even those that did, had no sign announcing them. Furthermore, none of the buildings had numbers, as they were usually known by the name of their owners. This wasn't really much use when trying to find directions in any case, as these names were only known locally and sometimes by the post office. Whenever I took a taxi home I would just announce 'Selemanieh' and give directions as we neared my street. When I drew maps for visitors, it helped to add both the cake shop and the music shop on the corner. However, as it was Sunday these shops were shut, so they had been of no use to Mustapha.

As we walked along the street, Mustapha glanced appreciatively around him at the well-dressed Christian girls and remarked that he almost felt he was back in Paris. It was better than the area he was living in, as most women tended to dress in black.

'How much does it cost to rent an apartment here?' He asked. 'Could I find one, do you think?'

I laughed, remembering Layla's most recent remark. 'I think you'd have to change your name, Mustapha. This is a Christian neighbourhood.'

'You mean they wouldn't rent to a Moslem?'

'Never in a million years. Unless, of course, they didn't know you were Moslem.'

'I guess the same goes for the girls,' he sighed, as a particularly attractive brunette passed us. 'I mean, I guess they would not want to go out with a Moslem.'

'I think you'd have some difficulties there,' I agreed.

We walked towards the four-minaret mosque, Jama' Al-Tawhid, and Mustapha commented on it being in the middle of the Christian quarter. 'There must be Moslems living here,' he said.

'No, we call that the irritation mosque. See, it has been built right next to St. George's Church.' Being Sunday evening, both buildings were lit up and there was a huge crowd clustered about the church as parishioners entered and exited, chatting excitedly to friends as they did. The mosque was emptier with just a couple of men, their backs to the street, praying silently, alone. 'You should see the mosque come Friday lunchtime. People come from all over the city to pray here: even the courtyard is full.'

Along the main road fronting the mosque, crowds of boys and young men had set up stalls selling paper twists of watermelon seeds and sticky sweets, chewing gum and cigarettes. One boy had a large bucket filled with water and bits of floating ice, from which cans of soft drink peeped through. He had a towel handy to dry the cans off when one was requested.

There was a tea merchant too, wearing colourful red and black trousers and a vest over a white shirt, his head partly covered with a red Turkish cap. He carried a large contraption half over his back and half snug against his chest, looking rather like a large Scottish bagpipes. Around his hips was a wide belt with a wooden cup holder jutting out in front of him and several cups standing ready in it. He held two more cups in his right hand, banging them together like a pair of castanets. As we passed someone requested some tea and, on paying five pounds, received a small cup which the seller filled by holding the cup at arm's length and bending his body to aim one of the bagpipe-like nozzles in the direction of the cup. Miraculously, it filled with hot tea. As the purchaser finished his cup, the seller poured a little more tea into the cup, swirled it around to rinse it and poured the dregs onto the road. The cup was ready for the next customer.

We weaved our way through the large groups of walkers: girls strolling arm-in-arm, sometimes three abreast; husbands and wives strolling likewise, at times pushing a pram between them; older women in small groups, all dressed in uniform black with their heads uncovered, their hair carefully made up and all with bright gold crosses lying exposed on their chests. There were young men too, who eyed the girls in much the same way as Mustapha was doing. However, we appeared to be the only mixed group of 'girls and boys'.

We neared the corner of the restaurant street. The grassed and concreted median strip was crowded with people, some sitting and munching their way through ice creams, others pushing strollers around, weaving in and out between the saucer-shaped lights that decorated the narrow park. In the evening darkness the lights shone out red, green, yellow and blue, briefly illuminating animated children's faces as they screeched past, playing chase. Rows of cars were parked along each side of the park while their owners sat in one of the restaurants lining each side of the dual carriageway.

On the opposite corner to where we stood waiting for the lights to change was 'MidMac', a popular hamburger restaurant. It was decorated with a large golden arched 'M' that somehow reminded me of a popular chain of fast-food places that existed outside of Syria. The MidMac hamburgers were, in fact, quite good and were served with french fries. However, like all Syrian restaurants, even fast-food joints like MidMac, there was table service. MidMac also offered pizzas and ice creams and as it was the latter we were after, the suggestion was made that we stop there.

'No,' I insisted. 'Let's go down the road further. I don't want to go to MidMac. I'll tell you why when we sit down.'

We walked on past Wanas where groups of men sat alone outside, separated from passers-by only by large pot plants. On the upper levels of the outside terrace were tables of mixed groups of men and women and large numbers of children, as Wanas reserved the best seats for family groups.

Finally, we stopped at Ebla, another restaurant, and took a table outside. A tuxedoed waiter, wafer-thin, took our orders of drinks and ice cream and disappeared inside. Another, less formally dressed, placed a freshly laundered cloth over the table with a flourish and added a new box of tissues to cover a small cigarette hole near the centre of the cloth.

'So why couldn't we go to MidMac?'

'Well, I object to going there now,' I replied. 'Last month Malika and I were invited to the school graduation ceremony at the citadel.' The ceremony had been an incredible experience, as 15 high school students obtained their baccalaureates amid much pomp with the centuries' old citadel as a backdrop. 'Well, anyway, we decided to stop at MidMac's for something to eat before going up to the citadel. It was late Friday afternoon and MidMac was half empty. As we sat in the garden part a Bedouin family passed. There was a man, what looked like his wife, sister and three children. They were all clean and tidy, wearing typical village dress – you know, jalabiya and scarf, and the women were in brightly-coloured dresses, some tattoos on their faces, gold jewellery and scarves just covering their hair. They began to enter MidMac's garden. I mean, it seemed to me that they had come into town on a Friday afternoon, perhaps to do some shopping or whatever; it was a holiday for them after all, and the father obviously wanted to give them a treat of an ice cream. Sure, MidMac is much more expensive than the street stalls, but the family didn't look poor and I'm sure the man knew how much MidMac would cost. Well, one of the waiters went up to the family and told them to leave. You should have seen the expression on the children's faces, it was a real disappointment. I felt sorriest for the father. He looked really embarrassed and I felt so angry with the waiter. Anyway, I refuse to go back, if MidMac is going to be so snotty.'

'Did you say anything to the waiter?'

I looked rather sheepish. 'I wanted to, but you know how it is. I am a foreigner and I didn't really dare.' I'd regretted not doing so ever since, but there was no real changing the attitudes of the people in Selemanieh. MidMac was run by Christians and they wanted only Christians as customers. Moslems would be tolerated if they were dressed and behaved appropriately – Malika was a Moslem, after all – but Bedouin or villagers, they just did not look the part. They were different and were despised, unless they were doing some good, such as cleaning the streets or selling vegetables.

Another evening I visited friends of ours who lived near the 'irritation' Mosque. We stood outside on the balcony observing the movements of all the neighbours in the apartments opposite. Several of the minarets were just visible through the maze of buildings and while we discussed the neighbours the evening prayer call rang out around us. I smiled at the sound while my hostesses made faces and pretended to spit.

'Come on,' I teased them. 'The sound is beautiful.'

'Bleaugh. You don't mean that.' They looked astounded.

'No, really, I love the sound of the mosque,' I insisted.

'Bleaugh. You're weird. Moslems... yeaurch.'

However, I did manage in this instance to get the last laugh. These friends were typical Christian girls. They hated Moslems, would have nothing to do with Moslems and had rarely, perhaps never, conversed with a Moslem. They had grown up in the Christian quarter, gone to Christian schools and now worked in Christian companies. They had not, like Layla, had the opportunity to attend school with Moslems or work in a multi-cultural organisation like ICARDA. When I finally got them to our apartment at the same time as Mustapha and other Moslem friends they began the evening by ignoring the Moslems totally. As the evening progressed and they learned that Moslems were actually human beings they began to thaw. After leaving Syria I got a letter from Layla describing an evening out where these Christian girls actually paired with Mustapha and another Moslem friend for three-couple dinner date.

The Parting

My final weekend in Selemanieh had come. Earlier in the week, Layla had insisted on organising a farewell party, which of course meant that the actual food preparation would be left to me. However, in compensation she settled down to thoroughly clean our apartment while Sheila, a European girlfriend, and I took over the kitchen.

Around lunchtime our upstairs neighbours – the mother and her two daughters – turned up, ostensibly for a cup of coffee and to say 'goodbye', but the real purpose of their visit soon became apparent. They had heard about our forthcoming party, of course. The whole neighbourhood knew I was leaving as Layla had ordered a huge cake from the shop below us.

Although in the middle of a massive cooking operation, Arab hospitality required my presence in the living room to entertain our 'visitors'. I left Sheila to the cooking. Our visitors drank their coffee and smoked their cigarettes while politely inquiring after my plans for the immediate future. Then our neighbour set her coffee cup down and embarked on the real purpose of her visit.

'The other day my husband saw a black man and another man entering this apartment,' she began, in Arabic as she spoke no other language, 'and he has been planning to come and talk to you about this. We cannot have such people in our building. You should not be entertaining men in this apartment.'

I looked at Layla, only half understanding what had been said. In fact, I understood the words, but I could not believe them. Sure, Mahmoud, a Sudanese (and rather dark) visited our apartment, but he had been doing so ever since we moved in, 15 months earlier. Why the accusations now? Furthermore, although he had been several times recently, he had been alone. The last time he had come accompanied by someone had been several weeks earlier, when he and Ahmed, a Moroccan friend, had come to dinner. Of course, in Arabic 'the other day' can be translated to mean 'a long time ago', however I wondered what the real purpose of the accusation was. I guessed it was because of the planned party and because Layla was going to be left alone in the apartment from the following day.

Layla ignored the remark about the 'black' man and replied that she had many uncles and cousins who visited regularly, besides her father of course, and that she could hardly prevent them from visiting her.

'Well, my husband is concerned at the number and the sorts of men that seem to be visiting you. Of course, I told him that as Lynne was an ajinabieh it was normal for her to have male friends, but all this sort of thing should stop. He wants to speak to you about it.'

'We have been living here for 15 months. I don't understand why you are bringing this up now,' Layla replied. 'We have never caused any problems and we have never had any parties.'

'Well, I realise that, but my husband doesn't. We have to consider the reputation of the building. What are you going to do when Lynne leaves? Surely your parents aren't going to let you live here alone? Certainly, you can't have men visit you then. All these men, they are friends of Lynne, aren't they?'

Layla turned to me and wailed in English, 'Lynne, take me with you when you leave. I can't stand this.' She then turned back and gave some sort of assurance to our neighbour that she would be looking for someone to share the apartment, particularly as the price would be too high for her to pay on her own. She neglected to mention that she had been planning to ask a male cousin of hers to move in, already aware what the reaction would be to this piece of news. Earlier in the week I had expressed some misgivings myself as to the acceptability of having a man share her apartment. Layla had assumed that once it became known that her parents were happy, her cousin would be accepted. Now she wasn't so sure.

Sheila walked in at that moment and mumbled a hello. Our neighbours stared at her in wonder, as she is tall, blond and very shapely, and her clothing that day accentuated her breasts and rather large hips, considered extremely sexy by Arab men.

'Gosh, she is so beautiful,' our neighbour exclaimed. All accusations about unwelcome male visitors were forgotten, as questions darted concerning Sheila and her history. Shortly thereafter, our neighbours left us in peace.

To begin with I was rather indignant at their intrusion, in particular their accusations levelled at my friends.

'Well, let the husband come and talk to me. I told her that I would speak to her husband. I'll tell him how much business it is of his who we have as friends. Oh Lynne, how can you leave me here alone? Sometimes I hate this society. They are so petty.'

'I guess you'll have to rethink the possibility of having your cousin move in here. They would never accept a man in here.'

'I guess not. Even if he is a cousin, he still has one of those things.' We all began giggling.

'They will develop hernias if they find out that we haven't invited one black man to the party tonight, we've invited three,' I laughed, 'so say nothing of a handful of Moslems. Shall we post signs on the door welcoming Mustapha and Mohammed and Jihad?'

Layla laughed but sobered immediately. 'That is probably their biggest worry – that we would actually invite Moslems here.' We returned to the kitchen to prepare some lunch.

Later in the afternoon I had a meeting with Mahmoud, the 'black' man in question, as we had a few things to purchase together for the party. I told him the story and he laughed, although he was worried that the situation could prevent him from visiting Layla after my departure. He didn't want to get her into trouble.

'I rather think she would enjoy getting into trouble,' I replied.

For once the apartment stairs were empty and no-one saw us climbing up to the apartment. Outside the door of our apartment, I began a huge miming act, pretending to call upstairs to our neighbours, and pointing in an exaggerated fashion in Mahmoud's direction. Laughing, we turned the key and walked into the apartment, only to find the neighbours once again comfortably installed in the living room. The shock on their faces must have closely resembled my own. Layla, more in control of the situation – after all, she had been expecting Mahmoud to be with me – immediately jumped up to shake his hand and welcome him. At the same time, she introduced him to our neighbours, although omitted to actually divulge his name.

'Oh, you speak Arabic,' our diplomatic and polite neighbour said. 'How come?'

'I am from the Sudan,' he replied. 'We speak Arabic there.'

I called Mahmoud into the kitchen to help with preparations there, and as he quitted the living room, our neighbour asked Layla, 'Is he Christian?'

Therein lay the crux of the whole problem. Layla lied and felt full of remorse afterwards about it. Her brave words of standing up to the neighbours simply could not stretch to admitting she had Moslem friends.

Shortly afterwards our neighbours left with a short, unemotional goodbye. As they left they whispered to Layla that they thought Mahmoud's eyes were beautiful. It was a round-about way of stating that they accepted his presence in the building.

Poor Mahmoud. Thanks to me he had had to suffer several embarrassing moments in Syria. Once, some two years earlier, he had accompanied me on one of my overnight trips to the Bedouin out in the desert. The Bedouin had never seen an African before and were amazed at the colour of his skin, his crinkly hair and his super-white teeth. What amazed them even more was the fact that he spoke such good Arabic and the crowning touch was that he was Moslem, like themselves. Any charms I may have had vanished with his presence and he became the centre of attention for a few days. Two years later, the Bedouin still asked after him each time I visited them.

Mahmoud left to make a few more purchases and some of Layla's friends arrived armed with make-up and hairspray. Their task was to transform Layla and me into belles of balls. With much effort and about 25 kilograms of spray they achieved their objective, although I felt I looked like a Chinese doll. Layla vowed that she had had no idea that I was so attractive and looking at the mirror I didn't recognise myself. Still, it was my farewell party. I had to look properly Syrian for once.

Everyone arrived on time, even Nabil, who I had confidently expected would be hours late. He would never leave his bookshop before 10p.m., even when there was nothing to do except drink coffee and entertain passers-by. When I handed him the invitation to the party, which stipulated the debut at 8p.m., he informed me he would arrive at 10p.m.

'No, 8p.m.,' I said.

'Ten o'clock.'

'No, 9p.m.'

'Nine thirty,' he countered.

'Nine p.m.,' I insisted, and he agreed. After that, I passed the shop each day and yelled 'nine p.m.' into his ear. As extra insurance, I asked Basel to pass by and pick him up. This he did, arriving at the same time as a group of Sudanese and a Tanzanian woman. Clattering on the stairs by earlier arrivals had opened all the apartment doors on the floors beneath our own and this large group of Syrians and Africans were greeted with amazed stares all the way up the 102 stairs to our apartment.

This diverse group of friends of 10 different nationalities (with only four people not speaking Arabic) settled down to ensure a marvellous party. They all laughed together at my expense over the invitation, as I had written it in Arabic. Layla had refused to correct it at all and I had tried to be poetic and get it to rhyme in limerick fashion. They got Layla to dig the invitation out and it was read out loud:

Aiwa, sa-athhab akhiran
wa sadikaty Layla mabsoota kathiran
biddha ta'amal haflah
biddna tijiy fee beitna youm al-jum'ah
as-sa'at 8 (al-mas'a ta'aban)

The translation was meant to be, roughly, 'yes I am leaving at last, and Layla is very happy. She wants to throw a party, we want you to come to our home on Friday, at eight o'clock (in the evening of course).'

'It took me three days to work out the last word,' someone exclaimed.

'Me too,' said another, "al-mas'a ta'aban,' what does that mean?'

I had made a big mistake. By interchanging two letters and adding the wrong ending, I had transformed 'taba'an' (of course) into 'ta'aban', which actually means 'tired'. The last phrase, instead of saying 'in the evening of course' had turned into 'the night is tired', which could be true had I meant eight o'clock in the morning, not necessarily an unusual hour for a Syrian party to finish!

'I wondered why Layla was so happy,' joked another.

Someone changed the cassette and Mahmoud dragged me up to dance, Arabic style, in the middle of the room. Everyone clapped and cheered and for the next hour or so pockets of people danced where there was room. We threw open the windows and the heat and noise blared out into the streets below.

As everyone calmed down to refill their glasses and glance longingly at the huge cake decorated in a multitude of marzipan flowers with the words 'farewell kiwi' written on it, Layla said, 'I've got to make a speech. I think I have to, don't I? I'd better.' She stood up, called for silence and, switching into English, began a long eulogy on my few qualities and many faults. She recounted special moments in our communal life, in particular a trip we had made together to England a couple of months earlier.

'It has all been due to Ben,' she said, 'who introduced us to each other. Sometimes I've praised him and sometimes I've cursed him.' We raised our glasses to Ben.

I could feel myself starting to cry and tried to pull myself into one piece again. Layla had finished her spiel, and everyone was looking at me for a response. I realised that a handful of our guests had not understood Layla's words and that three people would not understand Arabic. However, it seemed she had set a precedent. I launched into Arabic, trying to insult Layla but in reality, singing her praises and those of Ben. If I had anything to say against Ben, it was that he had caused this moment to come, when I had to say goodbye. After a few more words of thanks, to Layla and to Basel for the party, both Layla and I began to cry and we rushed into the kitchen.

'Our make-up, our make-up,' Layla cried, and we began to laugh again, drying up our China doll visages to return to our guests and cut the cake.

Finally, the guests stood up to leave and as they departed, hugging and kissing, the goodbyes got longer and more tearful. As the last one left, we both broke down totally in each other's arms, our make-up forgotten. We poured fresh drinks and, perched amongst bits of leftover cake and half eaten plates of food, began to talk and cry, all in a jumble.

'I need a cigarette,' Layla cried and she began to rummage through a number of cigarette packets lying around. Finally, she pounced on one that was only half empty.

'Bless the person who left this,' she said, pulling one out and lighting it.

'I'll join you,' I announced, taking one myself. We gradually stopped blubbing as we made an inroad into the packet and finished the bottle of wine. To accompany the cigarettes and wine we discussed each other's plans and projects, the conversation mostly centring around those creatures of great concern to our neighbours: men. We retired to bed with our problems unresolved, as always.

The next morning, I woke up early, unable to sleep. I packed up my bedding and dressed, almost in a daze. It seemed as if another person, not me, had entered my body during the night. I left the apartment to wander downtown and purchase my bus ticket to Amman in Jordan. (Fortunately for my emotional well-being, I had a conference to attend in Jordan prior to returning to Europe. It made the departure easier to cope with). I walked through Selemanieh as if seeing it for the first time. The sun had recently risen and sparkled yellow off the upper stories of the buildings. The deep blue sky peaked overhead. Early morning traffic had begun to circulate and some women could be seen hanging out their washing. An empty taxi tooted as he passed me, seeking a customer. An elderly man, stooped and grizzly, led a horse and cart along the curb, shovelling up the previous day's waste. A shopkeeper rolled up his metallic door and unlocked his shop. Another tradesman, his shop already open, sat in a ray of early morning sun drinking a small cup of coffee. I walked down through to Azizieh, stopping to admire the expensive clothes displayed in the corner windows of George Lahdo's shop, the first to display Adidas goods a couple of years previously. Rain fell from my eyes, I was leaving. My life in Syria had come to an end.

Epilogue

In 2012 much of the area in and around Selemanieh became a major battle ground. The 13th century souk and its 800 years of history was burned down. The stories coming from Syria these days are horrific and its images remind me of the destruction we saw in Beirut. Many of my friends have been able to get out of Syria, however I expect many people I knew have not managed to leave.

There have always been tensions in the Middle East – ever since the beginning of civilization. Perhaps in a few generations the so-called Arab Spring will be seen as the start of a new form of modernisation for this region and that something good came out of the death and destruction that has affected so many countries and so many people. I can only hope so. Certainly, the Syria I knew and loved has gone.

www.ingramcontent.com/pod-product-compliance
Ingram Content Group UK Ltd.
Pitfield, Milton Keynes, MK11 3LW, UK
UKHW041827200726
13854UKWH00002BA/647